JOURNAL FOR THE STUDY OF THE OLD TESTAMENT
SUPPLEMENT SERIES
183

Sheffield Academic Press

Lectures on the Religion of the Semites

Second and Third Series

William Robertson Smith

edited with an Introduction and Appendix by John Day

Journal for the Study of the Old Testament
Supplement Series 183

Copyright © 1995 Sheffield Academic Press

Published by Sheffield Academic Press Ltd
Mansion House
19 Kingfield Road
Sheffield, S11 9AS
England

Printed on acid-free paper in Great Britain
by Bookcraft Ltd
Midsomer Norton, Bath

British Library Cataloguing in Publication Data

A catalogue record for this book is available
from the British Library

ISBN 1-85075-500-0

CONTENTS

This volume is unique in the JSOT Supplement Series in that it contains neither a new work by a living scholar nor the republication of a classic work by a dead scholar. Rather, it contains the edited version of a hitherto unpublished work of a dead scholar, William Robertson Smith, one of the most outstanding biblical scholars and Semitists of the nineteenth century, the centenary of whose death in 1894 has recently been commemorated. The first series of Burnett *Lectures on the Religion of the Semites* has long been a classic work, but the second and third series of *Lectures* failed to appear in the author's own lifetime owing to the ill health of his latter years. The long forgotten manuscript was discovered by me in the Robertson Smith Archive in the Cambridge University Library in October 1991. Every attempt has been made to keep the author's *ipsissima verba* as much as possible, but considerable editing has been necessary, especially by way of filling out the references, which Smith tended to cite in abbreviated and cryptic form, and by way of stylistic improvements. To the edition of the manuscript I have appended at the beginning an Introduction and at the end a transcript of the press reports on the *Lectures* from *The Daily Free Press* and *The Aberdeen Journal*.

In preparing this work for publication I have been indebted to various individuals. Most of all I have to thank Carol Smith for her painstaking work in transcribing the edited version of Robertson Smith's manuscript, as well as the Introduction and press reports, on to a word processor, and for her patience in seeing the work through several drafts. Without her efforts, it may truly be said, Robertson Smith's work would never have seen the light of day. I also owe a debt of gratitude to Professor William Johnstone for the original suggestion that I search out the Robertson Smith archive in Cambridge in order to discover whether the manuscript of the second and third series of Burnett lectures still existed. I must further thank Dr Patrick N.R. Zutshi, Keeper of Manuscripts and Archives at the Cambridge University Library for granting me permission to receive xeroxes of the manuscript pages, and express my gratitude to the Syndics of the Cambridge University Library for permission to publish the manuscript. In addition I must acknowledge the kindness of Mrs Rachel Hart, an Archivist at Aberdeen, who procured for me copies of the press reports from *The Aberdeen Journal* from the Aberdeen University Library and instructed the British Library Newspaper Library to provide me with press reports from *The Daily Free Press*. Finally, I am indebted to Professor David Clines and Sheffield Academic Press for accepting this work for publication in the JSOT Supplement Series.

John Day
December, 1994

ABBREVIATIONS

BJRL	*Bulletin of the John Rylands University Library of Manchester*
BWANT	Beiträge zur Wissenschaft vom Alten und Neuen Testament
CIG	*Corpus Inscriptionum Graecarum*
CIS	*Corpus Inscriptionum Semiticarum*
ET	English translation
JRAS	*Journal of the Royal Asiatic Society*
JSOT	*Journal for the Study of the Old Testament*
JSOTSup	*Journal for the Study of the Old Testament*, Supplement Series
Praep. Ev.	*Praeparatio Evangelica*
TLZ	*Theologische Literaturzeitung*
ZDMG	*Zeitschrift der deutschen morgenländischen Gesellschaft*

INTRODUCTION*

The Discovery

In the Cambridge University Library there lies the manuscript of the last unpublished book by William Robertson Smith. To most scholars in the world this news will doubtless come as a big surprise, and they will no doubt wonder how such a thing could have remained unknown for so long.[1] But, as they say, fact is often stranger than fiction.

How did the discovery take place? It was William Johnstone who reminded me that Robertson Smith's classic work on *The Religion of the Semites*, originally published in 1889 (2nd edn, 1894; 3rd edn, 1927), was but the first of three courses of lectures given on that subject (as the Preface makes clear), and he wondered whether the manuscript of the remaining two series still existed in the Robertson Smith Archive in Cambridge. I told him I would go and have a look. So on 3 October 1991 I went to the Cambridge University library and discovered that the manuscript did indeed still exist. It is listed in the catalogue under 'William Robertson Smith' in the Manuscripts room, where one can order it. Behind the desk there is also a special folder, accessible on request, which gives a more detailed breakdown of the various parts of the Robertson Smith archive, including the contents of the second and third series of Burnett lectures. The relevant material is listed as ADD.7476.H69-77. (ADD.7476.H78 and 79 are also included with the material as belonging to the Burnett Lectures, but their content, though

---

*   An abbreviated version of this chapter appears as 'William Robertson Smith's hitherto Unpublished Second and Third Series of Burnett Lectures on the Religion of the Semites', in W. Johnstone (ed.), *William Robertson Smith: Essays in Reassessment* (JSOTSup, 189; Sheffield: Sheffield Academic Press, 1995), pp. 190-202.

1.   Writing of the second and third series of Burnett lectures, J.S. Black and G. Chrystal state in *The Life of William Robertson Smith* (London: A. & C. Black, 1912), p. 535, 'nothing of these now survives but the meagre press reports and the somewhat fragmentary notes from which he spoke.' This exaggerated statement doubtless discouraged anyone from seeking them out.

by Smith, is quite different, and seems to have been miscatalogued.) Originally the manuscript was in the library of Christ's College, Cambridge, the College at which Smith had been a professorial Fellow, and which still has his books, but it was given to the Cambridge University Library by the Master and Fellows of Christ's College in 1954.

The material relating to the Burnett lectures is as follows. All is in handwritten form, unless specifically indicated otherwise below.

ADD.7476.H69	Second series, lecture 1. 'Feasts' .
H69A	Typescript of H69
H70	Revised version of 'Feasts'.
H70A	Typescript of H70
H71	Further revised version of 'Feasts'.
H71A	Typescript of H71
H72	Second series, lecture 2. 'Priests and the Priestly Oracle'. (Includes 'with H72', a shorter variant version of the same lecture.)
H73	Second series, lecture 3. 'Priests (contd), Diviners, Prophets'.
H74	Third series, lecture 1. 'Semitic Polytheism (1)'.
H75	Third series, lecture 2. 'Semitic Polytheism (2)'.
H76	Third series, lecture 3. 'The gods and the world: Cosmogony'.
H77	Fragmentary notes relating to Smith's research for the third series of Burnett lectures.

It was by chance that I discovered that there were also extensive press reports on the lectures, for in the Robertson Smith Archive I found a press cutting on one of the lectures, that on Feasts, from *The Daily Free Press*. This made me suspect that there might be press reports on the others. Mrs Rachel Hart, an Archivist at Aberdeen University, established that all the second and third series of lectures (given in 1890 and 1891) were reported in *The Daily Free Press*, and also in another newspaper, *The Aberdeen Journal*. *The Aberdeen Journal* is available on microfilm at Aberdeen University Library, and extracts were obtained for me by Mrs Hart from a reader/printer. Mrs Hart also kindly got in touch with the British Library Newspaper Library, instructing them to make copies of the other five *Daily Free Press* reports that I needed. Although this newspaper is held in its original form at Aberdeen, it is too large to photocopy. The only way of obtaining copies for these would be by having negatives printed. This would have been very expensive. She established that the British Library Newspaper

Library had microfilms and so they were able to provide me with extracts from a reader/printer. I am indebted to Mrs Hart for procuring copies of these press extracts for me. From our vantage point today it is remarkable, not only that the lectures were reported on at all—in two newspapers—but that they were reported in such detail. This is clearly evidence of the high esteem in which Robertson Smith was held in Scotland, in particular in Aberdeen. Moreover, the press reports speak of large audiences at the various lectures. The text of the various press accounts of the lectures is provided in an Appendix at the end of this volume.

Editing and Publication

It soon became apparent that publication of the lectures would be desirable. In order to facilitate this it was necessary to obtain photocopies of all the relevant material, and the Cambridge University Library kindly provided these for me in January, 1992. Although I had to ask special permission for the photocopies to be made, there was fortunately no problem, as the pages were unbound, and there was therefore no danger to the manuscript. I am grateful to Dr Patrick N.R. Zutshi, Keeper of Manuscripts and University Archives, for granting permission for this. For permission to publish the manuscript I make acknowledgement to the Syndics of the Cambridge University Library.

The lectures required a lot of editing. As already indicated, apart from the first one on 'Feasts' (2.1), which exists in several redactions, the lectures are all in handwritten form. On occasion there were problems in deciphering Smith's handwriting, though usually his copperplate style was fairly easy to read. The really time-consuming thing was that Robertson Smith tended to give scholarly references in an abbreviated and often cryptic form, so that a lot of hard work was involved in tracking them down, mostly in the Bodleian. But with months of per-severance I have largely succeeded in locating the references. This involved, *inter alia*, searching out a considerable number of obscure classical Greek and Latin texts, dusty old nineteenth-century tomes in English, French and German, and also Syriac and Arabic works. Just to mention this gives an idea of Robertson Smith's incredibly wide-ranging erudition. But it was not only the references which proved a headache— the body of the text itself required a lot of editing. Surprisingly, Robertson Smith had a tendency of not writing in commas. More importantly, sometimes material existed only in note form. In general the third series is in a better state than the second series. The reader is directed to pp. 31 and 32 for examples of reproductions of pages which were particularly easy and particularly difficult to edit respectively.

In reading this edition of Robertson Smith's hitherto unpublished lectures, the reader may rest assured that I have endeavoured to keep to his *ipsissima verba* as much as possible. However, in the light of the above comments, it should be noted that this has not been entirely possible. Footnotes and references have been filled out, notelike material has been converted into proper sentences, citations from Semitic and classical languages have been transliterated and often translated, many commas have been added and other punctuation improvements made, other stylistic improvements have been introduced, and finally, the whole has been made to cohere with the conventions of Sheffield Academic Press.

In summer 1992, Carol Smith agreed to put my edited version of the manuscript on a word processor. One Smith thus facilitated the publishing of another! I can honestly say that, without Carol's assistance, Robertson Smith's unpublished lectures would not be seeing the light of day. Carol has occasionally been able to decipher words that had been incomprehensible to me, as well as adding a few more commas to what I had already introduced! She has also undertaken other tasks beyond the call of duty in connection with this work.

For agreeing to publish the lectures, together with my Introduction and the press reports, I am indebted to Professor David Clines and Sheffield Academic Press.

Earlier References to the Lectures

Not surprisingly, since the lectures have never previously been published, earlier references to them are few in number. The most informative is in J.S. Black and G. Chrystal, *The Life of William Robertson Smith*, which (apart from the original press reports) offers the only account of their content prior to the present volume. However, the synopsis is only brief, and although summarizing all three lectures of the second series (pp. 525-27), it only deals with the last of the third series (pp. 535-37).[2] Black and Chrystal also usefully set the composition of the

---

2.   Pp. 537-38 continue with further reflections by Black and Chrystal and also contain a brief reference to the speeches which followed at the end of Robertson Smith's final lecture.

lectures in the context of Smith's life. We learn, for example, that in addition to his general state of ill health, his father had died on 24 February, 1890, less than a week before he started delivering his second series.[3] This explains the cryptic allusion in *The Aberdeen Journal*'s report on the first lecture, to the fact that 'they were all aware that during the last few days other reasons had prevented him giving the attention that he ought to the subject.'[4] However, as already noted,[5] Black and Chrystal's exaggerated references to the fragmentary nature of the lectures probably had the effect of discouraging further interest in them.

Understandably, there are also very brief references to the second and third series of Burnett lectures at the beginning of the various editions of the first series of lectures on *The Religion of the Semites*. In addition to the allusion in the preface to the first edition, a note to the second edition by J.S. Black states that Smith's ill health from 1890 onward made it impossible for him to prepare them for publication. In the Introduction to the third edition (p. xxviii), S.A. Cook reiterates this, and briefly refers to their argument, noting the synopsis in the *Life of William Robertson Smith*.

However, we know that hopes were expressed for their publication by T.M. Lindsay[6] and, more significantly, by the German Old Testament scholar K. Budde, in a review of the second edition of *The Religion of the Semites*.[7] Budde's remarks were translated into English and reported in *The British Weekly*[8] and will be repeated here.

> The *Theologische Literaturzeitung* of Saturday last gives the foremost place to a review by Prof. Budde of the new edition of the late Robertson Smith's Lectures on the Religion of the Semites. After noting the points of difference between the new edition and the old, Prof. Budde goes on: 'The reviewer's duty might end here, but the fellow labourer has more he must say. First of all he must in the name of many express sorrow at the irremediable loss sustained in the death of the man who has given us so

3. Black and Chrystal, *The Life of William Robertson Smith*, p. 525.

4. See below, p. 115.

5. Above, p. 11 and n. 1.

6. T.M. Lindsay, 'Pioneer and Martyr of the Higher Criticism: Professor William Robertson Smith', *The Review of the Churches* 6 (1894), p. 42.

7. K. Budde, Review of W.R. Smith, *Lectures on the Religion of the Semites* (1st series, 2nd edn), in *TLZ* 20, no. 22 (26 October, 1895), cols. 553-54.

8. K. Budde, 'British Table Talk', in *The British Weekly* 19, no. 470 (31 October, 1895), p. 21. I am indebted to Professor William Johnstone for drawing my attention to this as well as the works cited in nn. 6 and 7.

much, and who might have been expected still to enrich us in many ways. This last work of his, taken up five years ago with almost general head-shaking, has in a short time produced the profoundest effect, and has almost imperceptibly, yet most thoroughly, revolutionized accepted views in the department of Old Testament study. It is because of Smith's results that we are to-day taken so severely to task as heretics. But his deeply Christian character, which he preserved through severe trials and sufferings, his firm belief in Divine Revelation, which he maintained intact in spite of every onslaught, must be accepted as proof that such investigations and views as his were do not lead men away from the well of truth, but serve to bring them nearer to it. Just, however, because of the greatness of our debt to him as a teacher, we are bound to express the earnest wish that nothing of his may be kept back which could help us on further. The book now before us contains only the first of three courses of lectures on the comprehensive subject. Prof. Smith was enabled to deliver the second and third courses in March, 1890, and December, 1891. Even if he was not permitted to make those lectures ready for the press, still the scientific may claim to be put in possession of what the hearers of the lectures obtained. In reply to an enquiry of mine about the second and third courses, the editor of this volume, Mr. J.S. Black, sent me very kind information, which, however, does not unfortunately sound encouraging. "His health," so he writes, "was at that time anything but good, and did not permit him to prepare as carefully as he would have done in days of health. For this reason he spoke practically *extempore*, as he could well do. His notes, which have been put into my hands, make it possible, indeed, to discern the line of his argument and the main grounds on which he based it. Yet they are in many respects far removed from what he himself would have liked to put before the public. How far and in what shape it would be possible, in view of their evidently incomplete and unfinished state, to publish them for the benefit of the learned world, and that without doing violence to the respect due to the memory of the dead is a matter which I am still pondering, and which I am consulting with other friends of Prof. Robertson Smith." In the name of German workers in the same department, I believe I may express the entreaty that these things may be considered in no timid spirit, and the assurance that as far as *we* are concerned there need be no fear of detriment to W.R. Smith's memory. What has already been published as his work would have been in our estimation a very great deal. It seems only natural in this age of shorthand, to ask whether, in a class which must surely have been a large one, there could have been no one who took down the words of so eminent a teacher, so that from such a report the thread might be derived with which to connect the autograph notes? In any case, let us have what can be given, and let our thanks be counted upon beforehand.'

The most bizarre allusion to the lectures is, however, also the most recent, and appears in an essay on 'Scottish Philosophy and Robertson Smith' by George E. Davie.[9] He writes (p. 139):

> Robertson Smith, indeed, died two or three years [*sic*] after his first series of lectures after a long illness and without being able to do more than give a programme for the second and third series, but the characteristic clarity of the notes he has left both for these and other things, enable us to chart with some confidence his chief lines of explanation and self-justification both in social anthropology and in religious philosophy.

Unfortunately, Davie's account of what was to be in the lectures is totally erroneous and he clearly had no reliable knowledge of their actual content, since he curiously claims (pp. 139-40) that Robertson Smith was going to discuss the clash between African sorcery and Christianity and argue that the 'limitation in our knowledge of the human mind and its workings does not rule out belief in transcendent or supernatural influences'! Ironically, it was in the very year of the publication of Davie's essay that my rediscovery of the manuscript of Robertson Smith's unpublished lectures occurred, thus revealing their true content.

The Lectures

After this necessarily extended Introduction, I must now get down to a consideration of the lectures themselves. They were delivered in the Upper Hall of Marischal College, Aberdeen University, the second series in March, 1890 and the third series in December, 1891, as follows:

Second Series
- (1) *Feasts.* Afternoon of Saturday, 1 March, 1890.
- (2) *Priests and the Priestly Oracle.* Afternoon of Monday, 3 March, 1890.
- (3) *Priests (contd), Diviners, Prophets.* Afternoon of Tuesday, 4 March, 1890.

Third Series
- (1) *Semitic Polytheism (1).* Afternoon of Thursday, 10 December, 1891.
- (2) *Semitic Polytheism (2).* Afternoon of Saturday, 12 December, 1891.

9.   See G.E. Davie, *The Scottish Enlightenment and other Essays* (Edinburgh: Polygon, 1991), pp. 139-41.

(3)   *The Gods and the World: Cosmogony.* Afternoon of Monday, 14 December, 1891.

2.1. *Feasts*

Three different drafts of this lecture are in existence, and each in turn is attested in both handwritten manuscript and typescript. H69 and H69A is the first, which is a rather long and indigestibly detailed series of notes. The second, H70 and H70A, which reads far more fluently, was the text delivered orally as the actual lecture, as is obvious from the press summaries. But it is clear that H71 and H71A make up Smith's latest version, and so should be regarded as the 'canonical' version. It incorporates much (though not all) of the material in H70 and H70A, but expands it with details on the New Moon and Sabbath, in addition to the sections on the Harvest Feast and the Calendar, which already existed in H70 and H70A. In the edition printed in this volume I have used H71 and H71A as the basic text, and have been able to fill out the footnotes with the help of the detailed material in H69 and H69A.

The already published first series of lectures centred on sacrifice. In beginning the second series it was natural that Smith first of all turned his mind to feasts, the context in which many sacrifices occurred. In addition to an introductory section, Smith has sections on Calendars, New Moon feasts, the Sabbath, and the Harvest Feast. I shall refer here to some of the more interesting points raised.

With regard to Passover, Smith emphasizes that the month of Nisan, in which Passover took place, was also sacred to other Semites. He mentions the Arabian sacrifices in the month of Rajab, and similarly in Cyprus on 1 April a sheep was offered to Astarte (Aphrodite) with ritual of a character evidently piacular. At Hierapolis, in Syria, in like manner, the chief feast of the year was the vernal ceremony of the Pyre, in which animals were burnt alive. And again, among the Harranians, the first half of Nisan was marked by a series of exceptional sacrifices of piacular colour. Traces of the sacredness of the month of Nisan are found also at Palmyra and among the Nabataeans. Smith also mentions the Babylonian New Year festival as being at this time.

Robertson Smith argues interestingly that the harvest festivals would originally have been celebrated at different times, according to the precise time of the harvest. Thus, for example, he notes that in the Philistine plain 'harvest begins about the middle of April or a week later, while at Hebron the first corn is not cut till about the beginning of June'.

Eventually, of course, the timing of the various festivals came to be fixed astronomically. Contrast the simple reference to the month of Abib for Unleavened Bread in the earliest calendars (Exod. 13.4; 23.15; 34.18; Deut. 16.1).

Perhaps the most interesting and original section of this lecture is at the end, where Robertson Smith attempts to find festal connections with the dates given in connection with Noah's flood. He notes that in P the flood begins on 17 Iyyar (Gen. 7.11), cf. Bērūnī, who reports that the heathen Syrians keep the 17th day of each month sacred because of the flood. 17 Iyyar was the date of a festival at Edessa, the Pannychis (cf. Joshua Stylites, *Chronicle*, 27 and 30): there were also seven days of celebration previously, cf. in J the seven days of preparation before the flood, Gen. 7.4. And among the Harranians 17 Iyyar was the feast of *Bāb at-Tibn*. In Lucian of Samosata, *De Dea Syria* 13, there are two annual feasts at Hierapolis in which water from the 'sea' is poured on the floor of the temple and descends into the chasm, through which the flood disappeared. Melito, in his 'Oration', says that the rite was to prevent the demon of the well from rising to destroy men. So far as I am aware, no one has investigated the possible festal connections of the flood dates to which Robertson Smith drew attention. Clearly someone should do so, as there may conceivably be some point in his observations.

2.2. *Priests and the Priestly Oracle*

This lecture exists in two different redactions. The first is the lecture that Robertson Smith actually delivered (cf. newspaper reports), which is still preserved (catalogued as 'with 72'). The other is the generally fuller, revised version, which is the version printed here (H72). Some of the interesting material about Phoenician parallels to Israelite priestly dress etc. appears both at the end of this revised form of the lecture and in briefer form at the beginning of the next lecture, 'Priests (contd), Diviners, Prophets'. In order to preserve the fuller version of this I have used that given at the end of 'Priests and the Priestly Oracle', but in order that the lengths of the chapters should not be excessively lopsided I have included it at the beginning of that on 'Priests (contd), Diviners, Prophets'. For this lecture Robertson Smith was able to draw on material from his article 'Priest' in the *Encyclopaedia Britannica*.[10] He

10. W.R. Smith, 'Priest', in *Encyclopaedia Britannica* XIX (Edinburgh: A. & C. Black, 9th edn, 1885), pp. 724-30.

defines a priest as 'a sacred minister, whose stated business is to perform on behalf of the community certain public ritual acts, especially sacrifices'.[11] He notes that in the earliest period the performance of priestly actions was not limited to a special sacerdotal class, but could be undertaken by members of the laity, especially leaders of society. Thus, the law of the altar in Exod. 20.22-26 is spoken to the people, not the priests; sacrifices are offered by Gideon and Manoah, and by kings such as Saul, David and Solomon, and Jeroboam burns incense. Also, David's sons are said to be priests, which Smith interestingly compares with the Tyrian custom of choosing the chief priests from the royal family. He even speculates that David may have imitated Tyre in this regard.

With regard to the royal participation in sacrifice, Smith denies that the monarchs were actually consecrated priests. Smith's view has sometimes been maintained by scholars subsequently, but one wonders how it can be reconciled with Ps. 110.4, where it is said of the Davidic king, 'You are a priest for ever after the order of Melchizedek.'

The Semitic country with the least developed priesthood was Arabia. Here the priesthood was hereditary in the family which owned the sanctuary, and this was often a noble family. In some cases the priestly family was of a different tribe from that of the tribal area in which the sanctuary was located, a relic of earlier inhabitants. That such priests were able to maintain their position may be explained by comparing 2 Kgs 17.24-28, where the Mesopotamian immigrants to Samaria required a Hebrew priest to teach them the law of the god of the land.

Smith notes that, contrary to the impression that might be gained from the Priestly legislation in the Pentateuch, the divine oracle was not confined to the Urim and Thummim of the Aaronite High Priest. For example, the ephod and teraphim could have this role, as we see from Judg. 18.17-20 and Hos. 3.4. However, from the time of Moses the Tabernacle and the Ark were the great seat of God's decisions. What the original relation of the Ark and Tabernacle was we do not know, but we should note that in the oldest narrative the two are not mentioned together. The notion that the Ark contained the written Law is late, but Smith speculates that originally it was the seat of the oral Law, that is, the priestly oracle, perhaps the ephod.

---

11. In the lecture originally delivered Smith quoted the epistle to the Hebrews 5.1 and 10.11 to explicate the role of the priest. Cf. the press report in *The Daily Free Press*, below, pp. 116-17.

2.3. *Priests (contd), Diviners, Prophets*

Continuing with the subject of priesthood, one interesting point that Robertson Smith makes is the close resemblance between Israel's developed priesthood and that of the Canaanites. For example, the priests were all in white, wearing linen: the Hebrews took this over from the Canaanites (Phoenicians) but it is ultimately Egyptian. Other parallels are the wearing of a cap on the head (cf. Lucian of Samosata, *De Dea Syria*, 42) and the fact that the priests officiated barefoot—so at Gades (cf. Silius Italicus, *Punica*, 3.28) and among the Hebrews, according to a tradition which is no doubt sound, and which declared that no one was to wear shoes in the Temple.

Another topic with which Robertson Smith deals is that of divination (cf. Deut. 18.10-11). This was a subject which he had already treated a few years earlier in two articles in the *Journal of Philology* in 1885.[12] In his lectures, Smith emphasizes that certain heathen practices were absolutely forbidden to the Hebrews; others were forbidden only when conducted in the name of other gods than Jehovah. Of this latter kind were dreams and visions. The former, acts absolutely forbidden to the Hebrews, included divination pure and simple, and magic, for example wizards, charms, and auguries.

The main part of this chapter deals with Prophecy. This, of course, was a subject which Smith had treated on previous occasions: in his early theological essays and in his lectures on prophecy delivered to his classes in Aberdeen,[13] in his well-known book on *The Prophets of Israel*, published in 1882, and in his article 'Prophet' in the 9th edition of the *Encyclopaedia Britannica*.[14] As J.S. Black and G. Chrystal put it,[15]

> His conclusion as expounded to the hearers of the Burnett Lectures, was as it had always been, that all purely 'naturalistic' explanations of the development of Hebrew prophecy were doomed to failure, and that the uniqueness of the revelation recorded in the canonical scriptures must be recognised.

12. W.R. Smith, 'On the forms of divination and magic enumerated in Deut. XVIII.10,11', *Journal of Philology* 13 (1885), pp. 273-87, and 14 (1885), pp. 113-28.

13. W.R. Smith, 'Prophecy and Personality', 'The question of prophecy in the critical schools of the continent', 'The fulfilment of prophecy', and 'Two lectures on prophecy', in J.S. Black and G. Chrystal (eds.), *Lectures & Essays of William Robertson Smith* (London: A. & C. Black, 1912), pp. 97-108, 163-203, 253-84, and 341-66.

14. W.R. Smith, 'Prophet', in *Encyclopaedia Britannica* XIX (Edinburgh: A. & C. Black, 9th edn, 1885), pp. 814-22.

15. Black and Chrystal, *The Life of William Robertson Smith*, p. 527.

Only the other day, Robertson Smith says, a reviewer had criticized him for saying that it was a mistake to suppose that the Old Testament could only have been produced by the Hebrews. 'In point of fact', Smith says,

> there is not the smallest historical evidence that anything like Amos, Isaiah, or Jeremiah was produced by any of the heathen Semites, or even that any branch of the Semites rose to a religious condition in which such prophecy would have been possible. [Applause from the audience!]

In the sense that prophecy was simply prediction, 'there was prophecy in all Semitic, nay, in all ancient nations.' But this is not the Old Testament understanding, and

> If the proof of the unique character of the Old Testament revelation is to be rested on a comparison between the fulfilled predictions of the Old Testament and those recorded in the literature of other nations, the victory of the Bible will not be very decisive.
>   Again…if the mark of a prophet is to speak in ecstasy, pouring forth mechanically a revelation in which his reason has no part, prophecy is not confined to Israel, nor to the Semites; for to speak in ecstasy or frenzy is the mark of the Greek *mantis* as well as of the Syrian *qāṣem* and the Arabic *kāhin*… But it is certain that Amos and Isaiah did not speak mechanically in a frenzy… The mechanical theory is not biblical, but flows from Philo's half-heathen philosophy of religion.

He goes on to dismiss Mohammed as an unoriginal political manipulator, and concludes, 'Old Testament prophecy remains, before as after investigation, a thing unique in the world's history.' (Applause!) It is in this chapter, I think, that we see most of Smith the Christian theologian as opposed to the detached student of comparative religion.

3.1. *Semitic Polytheism (1)*

The central emphasis of this chapter is the local sphere of influence of the god, as Robertson Smith understands it: the energy of the god had its centre at the sanctuary, and the god was less powerful at a distance from the sanctuary. When people extended their borders the god went with them, so sanctuaries might be multiplied. To illustrate his thinking, Robertson Smith cites the example of Tyre. The Tyrians set up temples and altars to Melqart wherever they went, but it was still deemed a sacred duty to send gifts of homage to the temple of the mother city (cf. Diodorus Siculus, 20.14).

Smith notes that among the Greeks two conceptions loosened the local connection of the gods: (i) the notion of a common dwelling of the gods on Olympus (in addition to their local dwellings), and (ii) the identification of the gods with astral and other heavenly bodies (e.g. the sun). He asks whether anything comparable happened with the Semites. With regard to (i), he notes that some have seen in Isa. 14.13 evidence of a Semitic Olympus, but he denies that this tells us anything of Hebrew belief. With regard to (ii), Smith admits that astral deities play a great part in Babylonian religion, but how far the Western Semites identified their gods with astral powers *before* the Assyrian period is hard to say. He states that not all the highest gods were astrally identified, and he claims that the Baals were telluric rather than heavenly powers. (At this point we may interject that the Ugaritic texts have shown, against Smith, that Baal was a heavenly god, even if not an astral one.) But even in the later period when the more famous gods were generally conceived as heavenly powers, the conception that their power radiated from a local centre persisted unimpaired. He compares the Baetocaece inscription, which states that the heavenly Zeus's power proceeds from that village.[16]

Robertson Smith's emphasis on the local character of the deity has tended to recede since the discovery of the Ugaritic texts, which reveal Canaanite gods such as El and Baal to have been universal deities of cosmic power. But it seems to me that there was a local aspect to them which has been overshadowed in more recent scholarship. One may compare the Old Testament allusions to the Baals of different localities, such as Baal-Hermon (Judg. 3.3; 1 Chron. 5.23) and Baal-Gad (Josh. 11.17, 12.7, 13.5).

In the final pages of this chapter Smith has a section on portable sanctuaries. I will not summarize all his arguments here, except to note that he thinks that they (e.g. the Ark) do not have a nomadic back-ground, since there is less trace of such an institution in Arabia than any other part of the Semitic world. He notes that the Ark is not carried back by Hebrew tradition to patriarchal times. It is much more likely that portable symbols of the godhead first arose among the settled Semites and in connection with the religion of the army at war. He compares Diodorus Siculus, 20.25 and Polybius, 7.9 for the idea of portable sanctuaries and images among the Carthaginians in war.

---

16. P. Le Bas and W.H. Waddington, *Voyage archéologique en Grèce et en Asie Mineure* (Paris: Didot, 1870), no. 2720a.

3.2. *Semitic Polytheism (2)*

In this lecture Robertson Smith begins by noting an interesting difference between the characteristic Greek and Semitic attitudes. As an example of the Greek attitude, he cites the conduct of Alexander the Great, who on capturing Tyre sacrificed to its god Melqart. By way of contrast, when a Semitic state was at war, the gods were at war also: sanctuaries would be destroyed and idols would be carried off as trophies. Smith notes, for example, that this was the standing practice of the Assyrians. David's capture of the idols of the Philistines (2 Sam. 5.21) was therefore typical of Semitic practices.

Robertson Smith goes on to claim that 'beyond question the worship of many gods side by side, where it occurs among the Semites, is due to the combination in one state of elements that are not homogeneous.' He illustrates this thesis by showing how polytheisms in the Semitic world could develop, for example, from commercial relations between different states.

Interestingly, Smith is of the view that from the time of Elisha onwards,

the mass of the Israelites, [though] prone to idolatry and ready to accept all the corruptions of Canaanite heathenism if they were disguised under the name of Jehovah worship, were little disposed to tolerate a foreign god by the side of Jehovah.

The exception was in the last days of the southern kingdom, when gods such as the Assyrian astral deities got a hold on Judah. Smith thus touches on a debate that still reverberates today about the extent of polytheism among the pre-exilic Israelites. It would appear that Robertson Smith's position is closer to that of J. Tigay than of those such as E.W. Nicholson,[17] who would see the Israelites as essentially polytheistic at that time.

Only three years before Smith's lectures were delivered, an important book on Semitic polytheism had been published by the German Old Testament scholar Friedrich Baethgen, *Beiträge zur semitischen Religionsgeschichte* (Berlin: H. Reuther, 1888), a work still not without interest, in spite of its age.

---

17. J. Tigay, *You shall have no other gods* (Atlanta: Scholars, 1986); E.W. Nicholson, 'Israelite Religion in the pre-exilic period', in J.D. Martin and P.R. Davies (eds.), *A Word in Season: Essays in honour of William McKane* (JSOTSup 42; Sheffield: JSOT Press, 1986), pp. 3-34.

Smith takes issue with what he regards as Baethgen's tendency (pp. 12-16) to exaggerate the polytheism of Israel's neighbours, especially Moab and Ammon. Whereas Baethgen had found evidence of four Moabite deities—Chemosh, Ashtar-Chemosh (interpreted as Chemosh's spouse on the Moabite stone), Baal-peor (Num. 25.1-3), and Nebo—Smith saw only two, Chemosh and his spouse, Ashtar-Chemosh. Smith claims, rightly, that Nebo, in the name Mt Nebo, is unlikely to be the name of the Babylonian god Nebo worshipped by the Moabites, but is more likely (as T. Nöldeke[18] maintained) cognate with the Arabic word *an-nabāwah*, meaning 'height'. But Smith is less convincing in supposing (with Jerome) that Baal-peor is to be equated with Chemosh. With regard to the Ammonites, Robertson Smith claims that there is no evidence for the worship of any god but Milkom (whom he calls Malkam). Baethgen himself had found little evidence for other Ammonite deities, but attributed this to the paucity of available sources. Baethgen would appear to have been right, given the Ammonite king's name *B'lyš'* found on a seal (probably = Baalis in Jer. 40.14).[19] Interestingly, this question too is still a live issue, since in 1993, at a conference in Bern in Switzerland, André Lemaire claimed that the Ammonites, Moabites and Edomites were essentially monolatrous,[20] not realizing that Robertson Smith had argued a fairly similar position 100 years ago, but for the reasons given above I regard this as improbable.

In the final section of this chapter Robertson Smith considers the question of the equation of Greek and Semitic deities. He notes, for example, that the Semitic god Melqart was equated with the Greek Heracles, the Semitic goddess Astarte was identified with the Greek Aphrodite, and the Semitic gods Resheph, Eshmun and El were equated with the Greek gods Apollo, Asklepios and Kronos respectively. But in this longish section Robertson Smith criticizes the tendency of scholars simply to read off the character of Semitic deities from their Greek equivalents. In particular, he devotes much space to the cases of Astarte and Aphrodite and Eshmun and Asklepios.

18. T. Nöldeke, review of F. Baethgen, *Beiträge zur semitischen Religionsgeschichte*, ZDMG 42 (1888), p. 470.
19. See the discussion and literature in L.T. Geraty, 'Baalis', in D.N. Freedman (ed.), *Anchor Bible Dictionary* I (New York: Doubleday, 1992), pp. 556-57.
20. A. Lemaire's arguments are published in 'Déesses et dieux de Syrie-Palestine d'après les inscriptions (c. 1000-500 av. n.-è.)', in W. Dietrich amd M.A. Klopfenstein, *Ein Gott allein?* (13. Kolloquium der Schweizerischen Akademie der Geistes- und Socialwissenschiften 1993; Freiburg: Universitätsverlag, 1994), pp. 142-45.

3.3. *The Gods and the World: Cosmogony*

In my view the most interesting chapter is this last one. One reason why it is interesting is that, already before Gunkel's *Schöpfung und Chaos in Urzeit und Endzeit* (Göttingen: Vandenhoeck & Ruprecht, 1895), it discusses the relationship between the biblical creation traditions in Genesis 1 and the Babylonian creation mythology in *Enuma elish*, the latter being reinforced by the Greek accounts of Babylonian cosmogony preserved in Damascius and Berosus. Smith writes, 'Without Damascius and Berosus the fragmentary tablets would hardly have been intelligible', something we tend to forget nowadays. It is interesting that already before Gunkel, Robertson Smith can write that 'most recent writers lay stress' on the parallelism between Genesis 1 and the Babylonian account—Gunkel's work was thus not a bolt from the blue. Smith, however, declares that this parallelism has been exaggerated. He notes that the Hebrews and Babylonians shared the idea of a solid domed firmament with the waters beyond it. In the Babylonian myth the chaos is productive; in the Bible it is only the raw material of creation from which the orderly elements of the cosmos are separated by the creative word of God. Robertson Smith is unable to find any greater parallelism between the two accounts than follows from the fact that the Hebrews and Babylonians shared similar conceptions of the universe.

With regard to the order of creation, Robertson Smith finds nothing beyond what one might expect from the necessities of the case. And some of the most striking features in the biblical story, for example the creation of light and the first growth of plants preceding the creation of heavenly bodies, cannot be shown to reappear in the Babylonian myth. In Berosus's story, indeed, the creation of the heavenly luminaries is mentioned after the death of the animals that cannot bear the light. For the present at least, until the blanks in the creation story are supplied, we cannot say with certainty that light shone in the Babylonian chaos before the sun was made, Smith says.

Interestingly, the question of the relationship between Genesis 1 and the Babylonian traditions has continued to be debated over the last century. And although many have supposed that there is some direct connection, Robertson Smith may well have been right to question this. As I have argued elsewhere,[21] Genesis 1 is probably dependent

21. Cf. J. Day, *God's Conflict with the Dragon and the Sea* (Cambridge: Cambridge University Press, 1985), ch. 1.

ultimately on Canaanite rather than Babylonian traditions.

In the second half of this chapter, Robertson Smith goes on to the subject of Phoenician cosmogony. He notes that the best established point, which appears in Mochus (in Damascius, 125C), and Eudemus (also in Damascius, 125C) is that the world came into being by the bursting in two of a cosmic egg. The egg, says Mochus, was broken into two and one piece became heaven and the other earth. This egg thus takes the place of the sea monster Tiamat in the Babylonian *Enuma elish*. How this egg was burst, Smith notes, is not clear, but Mochus speaks of an opener whom he calls Khousoros. The name Khousor also appears in Philo of Byblos as a god, the inventor of iron, etc. (in Eusebius, *Praep. Ev.*, 1.10.11). From our modern, post-Ugaritic viewpoint, Smith's observation here is exceedingly interesting, for in the Baal-Yam text, it is the craftsman god Kothar-and-Hasis—whose name clearly underlies that of Khousor or Khousoros—who makes the clubs with which Baal defeats Yam (the sea).

Robertson Smith continues by noting that the Phoenician accounts agree in making the egg or *'ôlām*, the father of the egg, be preceded by the winds and by a murky, turbid chaos, which is also called a mist or even Air. The primaeval world, *'ôlām*, seems to be conceived as condensed by the action of the winds on a thin, dark mist without limits. Here, Smith says, we have a view closely parallel to the brooding of the spirit of God on the face of the deep in Gen. 1.2. He is doubtless right in seeing some connection here, even though 'hovering' rather than 'brooding' is now generally agreed to be the correct rendering of the Hebrew *meraḥepet*. And if we render *rûaḥ* by 'wind' rather than 'spirit', as I maintain,[22] the parallel becomes even closer.

Another interesting parallel which Robertson Smith notes in this chapter is that between the list in Gen. 4.17-26 of those who were the first inventors of various features of human society and the comparable Phoenician account of such persons preserved in Philo of Byblos (in Eusebius, *Praep. Ev.*, 1.10.6-14). Attention has been drawn to these parallels in more recent years by U. Cassuto, James Barr and J. Ebach.[23]

---

22. Day, *God's Conflict with the Dragon and the Sea*, pp. 52-53.

23. U. Cassuto, *A Commentary on the Book of Genesis. Part I: From Adam to Noah* (Jerusalem: Magnes, 1961), pp. 230-37; J. Barr, 'Philo of Byblos and his "Phoenician history"', *BJRL* 57 (1974), p. 50; J. Ebach, *Weltentstehung und Kulturentwicklung bei Philo von Byblos* (BWANT 108; Stuttgart: W. Kohlhammer, 1979), pp. 330-52.

For example, in Gen. 4.17, 20-22, Cain is the first city-builder, Jabal the father of tent-dwellers and those who raise livestock, his brother Jubal of musicians, and Tubal-Cain is the first smith. Robertson Smith notes that the shepherd Jabal has perhaps his Phoenician parallel in Amynos and Magos, who introduced villages and flocks of sheep. Jubal may be compared with Sidon, the woman with an incomparable voice who first discovered melodious hymns. Smith notes one difference, however, in that Genesis lacks a story about the invention of fire, something which we do have in Philo of Byblos.

In the final section of this chapter Robertson Smith again anticipated some subsequent scholarship. He claims that Ezek. 28.12-19, with its depiction of Eden, the trees, the cherub and the other details, describes in great part the scenery of a Phoenician temple. The tree and the serpent, the cherubim and the flaming sword are all to be found at Tyre, and from these the Hebrew story borrows its imagery, though it puts a new meaning into it. The fiery stones are plainly the luminous pillars of Melqart, Smith says, and the holy mountain of God is the rock on which the temple stood. The flaming sword of Genesis 3 corresponds, he claims, to the lambent flame round the Tyrian tree. Although the specifically Tyrian connection which Smith puts forward seems questionable, I would note that Gordon Wenham[24] has recently argued that the imagery of Eden in Genesis 2–3 represents a temple, without knowing that Robertson Smith had already argued it a century earlier with regard to Ezekiel 28.

Robertson Smith concludes this lecture, and with it the final series of Burnett lectures, with words which emphasize that, for all the parallels between the Old Testament and its Semitic background, there is something unique about the Old Testament.

> All this shows that Phoenician and Hebrew legends covered much the same general ground, but the similarity in material details only brings into more emphasis the entirely different spirit and meaning. The Phoenician legends are bound up throughout with a thoroughly heathen view of god, man and the world. Not merely are they destitute of ethical motives, but no one who believed them could rise to any spiritual conception of deity or any lofty conception of man's chief end. The Hebrew stories in Genesis, looked at in their plain sense, contain much that is not directly edifying.

24. G.J. Wenham, 'Sanctuary symbolism in the garden of Eden story', in *Proceedings of the Ninth World Congress of Jewish Studies: Division A. The Period of the Bible* (Jerusalem: World Union of Jewish Studies, 1986), pp. 19-25.

They do not make the patriarchs models of goodness, but they never make religion involve the approbation of a lower morality or a low view of the deity. In them God communes with men without ever lowering himself to the level of man. He had no human passions or affections, for his love to his chosen people was raised far above the weaknesses of human preferences. Above all, he was the God of the world before he was Israel's God, while in all the Semitic legends the Demiurge himself was always, and above all, the local king.

The burden of explaining this contrast does not lie with us: it falls on those who are compelled by a false philosophy of revelation to see in the Old Testament nothing more than the highest fruit of the general tendencies of Semitic religion. That is not the view that study commends to me. It is a view that is not commended but condemned by the many parallelisms in detail between Hebrew and heathen story and ritual. For all these material points of resemblance only make the contrast in spirit more remarkable.

Robertson Smith's Use of Ancient Near Eastern (especially Assyriological) and Classical Sources

Robertson Smith, like Wellhausen, has been accused of concentrating on Arabian material and ignoring the newly made ancient Near Eastern discoveries of his time, especially the Assyriological data from Mesopotamia. One interesting and important point which emerges in the second and third series of Burnett lectures is the much greater attention to Assyriological and other ancient Near Eastern material which they contain compared to Smith's earlier works. As I noted earlier, he was fully aware of *Enuma elish* and the discussion about its relation to Genesis 1 before Gunkel's classic book. He knows and cites the works of leading Assyriologists such as P. Jensen and E. Schrader.[25] He cites Tiglath-Pileser III's annals with regard to the taking of foreign idols as trophies as characteristic of the Semitic attitude. He can quote the annals of Asshurbanipal. He can refer to the Babylonian and Assyrian Ishtar and notes a text describing the idol of Nana of Erech being carried off by the king of Elam. With regard to West Semitic texts, Robertson Smith is fully cognizant of the Moabite stone of king Mesha, he knows of the Moabite seal of Kemoshyeḥi, and quotes quite a number of inscriptions from *Corpus Inscriptionum Semiticarum*.

25. P. Jensen, *Die Kosmologie der Babylonier* (Strasbourg: K.J. Trübner, 1890); E. Schrader, *Die Keilinschriften und das Alte Testament* (Giessen: J. Ricker, 2nd edn, 1883), and (ed.), *Keilinschriftliche Bibliothek I-III* (Berlin: H. Reuther, 1889–90).

Another general observation which strikes any modern Old Testament and Semitic scholar perusing these lectures—and this is true also of the already published first series of lectures—is how amazingly learned Robertson Smith was in the ancient classical Greek and Latin sources, and the very good use he made of them in shedding light on the Semitic background of the Old Testament. Smith's pages are graced with references to such authors as Diodorus Siculus, Herodotus, Polybius, Homer, Lucian of Samosata, Philo of Byblos, Damascius, Berosus, Abydenus, Eusebius, Nonnos, Silius Italicus, Herodian, Marcus Diaconus and Jerome. Both because of the general decline in classical education and learning and as a result of the discovery of ancient Near Eastern texts such as those from Ugarit and Mesopotamia, Old Testament scholars today make little use of these classical sources. The experience of reading Robertson Smith and tracking down his references makes me feel that Old Testament and Semitic scholars should renew their attention to these classical sources, for on occasion they can be really illuminating.[26]

---

26. An example of an Old Testament scholar who has recently made good use of classical sources, in this instance in connection with the wider Semitic background of Israel's dietary laws, is W.J. Houston, *Purity and Monotheism: Clean and Unclean Animals in Biblical Law* (JSOTSup 140; Sheffield: JSOT Press, 1993).

Lecture I. Semitic Polytheism

It is very difficult for us to enter into the habit of thought

Do you remember the time when as children you first read the Old Testament History? And if so And do you remember being puzzled by what I well remember was the great puzzle of that history to me? Why were the Israelites so ready to go aside & worship other gods? What was there to attract them in the strange gods of their neighbours? I remind you of this difficulty now, not that I may answer the question, at least not at present, but because the very existence of such a difficulty is instructive as shewing how entirely remote our modern habits of thought are from those in which the polytheism of the ancient Semites had its root. He cannot even We all have our doubts and our temptations in matters of faith, but we cannot imagine ourselves tempted to believe in the Baalim & the Ashtaroth whose worship had so fatal an attraction for the ancient people of Jehovah.

It is This entire want of sympathy with the standpoint of Semitic heathenism makes a real is a grave obstacle to the scientific study of the subject. What we know of the Semitic gods & of the beliefs of their worshippers concerning them is all fragmentary & to piece these fragments together & build up from them a consistent account of Semitic polytheism as a whole it is above all things necessary that we should be able to put ourselves alongside of the way of thinking to which these strange deities were conceivable, credible & worthy of worship. If we carry our own modern and Christian ideas habits of religious thought into the study we shall be liable at every moment to put a false construction on the facts before us & draw inferences that the old heathen worshippers did not and could not draw.

Example of a page easy to edit.

ii.2

That the Eshmun of Sidon was the supreme god is I think made
probable by another circumstance. Renan found in the environs
of Cyprus an inscription of the second Christian century (Phén. p. 397)
according to Θρεπτίων Νείκωνος τοῦ Σωσίππου τοὺς δυὸ
λέοντας ΔΙΙ ΟΡΕΙΝῼ κατ' ὄναρ, ἐκ τῶν ἰδίων εὐσεβῶν
ἀνέθηκεν. The mountain Zeus at Sidon can hardly be any other god
than the Eshmun whose mountain sanctuary Eshmunazar built
and if Zeus is necessarily the supreme god. And that the great god of the
Sidonian mountain is Eshmun & no one else may be argued from
the lions dedicated to him

These two lions may be compared with the two golden gazelles in the Well
Zemzem & the two golden camels dedicated to Dhu Samā or a Homyarite
& to Dusares in an inscr. of Puteoli (Cf Nöld. ZDMG XXXVIII, 1884 p. 143)
They imply that there was some connection between the god & the lion. Now at Ascalon
according to Marinus (Vita Procli c. XIX Ἀσκληπιὸς λεοντοῦχος appears but
Ascalon & from the context appears to be the chief god there worshipped
The force of this argt is perhaps weakened by the existence of other lion gods
like the Γεννάῖος of Heliopolis Rel Sem, 156. If the Baal of Sidon has the lion as
the Astarte sits on the Bull this if the exact opposite of Hierapolis where the
goddess sits on the lion & the god on the bull. At any rate
Λεοντοπόλιον (in Africa) shews that the lion god is Baal. All this makes
Eshmun rather the lion killing Heracles of the patera Pietrobn. 189 than
the Cherub slaying youth (Iolaos!) – Cf also the lion
of Amathus Perrot iii.567 & the two אריה lions C.15. 103 dedicated to
Reshef-Hes

At Carthage the temple of Asclepius occupied the summit of the citadel
hill & was by far the most splendid in the town (Appian Pun.130) That
the Asclepius of Appian is Eshmun is generally accepted & confirmed by
CIS 252 where the temple of Eshmun is mentioned [Movers has argued
that he is the Iolaus of Hannibals oath Polyb VII.9 who appears as
third with the δαίμων Καρχηδονίων and Heracles but if conjectures
have place in such a matter) & his temple also held a chief place at
New Carthage Polyb X.10.8, so that he is evidently one of the greatest
Carthaginian gods. And here as at Sidon he is associated with
Astarte as the compound form עשתרתחם אשמנ CIS 243 shews

Second Series, Lecture 1

FEASTS

From an early date communal sacrifices began to be celebrated periodically, as well as on special occasions such as war. The example of the Arabs shows that periodical feasts began in the nomadic life; indeed, such sacrifices are even found in the hunting stage. Among the Arabs there were the spring sacrifices of the month of Rajab. Parallels in spring atoning sacrifices are found elsewhere. Thus, in Cyprus, on 1 April, a sheep was offered to Astarte (Aphrodite) with a ritual of a character evidently piacular.[1] Among the Harranians the first half of Nisan was marked by a series of exceptional sacrifices of piacular colour.[2] At Hierapolis, in like manner, the chief feast of the year was the vernal ceremony of the Pyre in which animals were burned alive in an antique ritual.[3] Traces of the sacredness of the month Nisan are also found among the Nabataeans and at Palmyra.[4] The Babylonian New Year festival was likewise at this time. The Hebrew Passover, which is also in Nisan, is older than the settlement in Canaan and presents antique features similar to those of the most primitive Arabian sacrifices. In the later forms of Semitic religion, as elsewhere among the civilized peoples of antiquity, we find an elaborate cycle of annual feasts—a sacred calendar. And we also find holy days—New Moons and Sabbaths based on the revolution of the moon. That the Sabbath is connected with the month will appear as we proceed.[5]

1. Lydus, *De Mensibus*, 4.45.
2. G. Flügel (ed.), *Kitâb al-Fihrist* (Leipzig: F.C.W. Vogel, 1871), p. 322.
3. Lucian, *De Dea Syria*, 49.
4. For the Nabataeans see W.R. Smith, *Religion of the Semites* (1st series, 1st edn; London: A. & C. Black, 1889), p. 387 n. 3 (= 2nd edn, 1894, p. 407 n. 1), and for Palmyra, see W.R. Smith, 'Palmyra', *Encyclopaedia Britannica* XVIII (Edinburgh: A. & C. Black, 9th edn, 1885), p. 199 n. 2.
5. [This paragraph, together with the footnotes, has been expanded with the help of Smith, *Religion of the Semites* (1st series, 1st edn), p. 387 (= 2nd edn, pp. 406-7).—J.D.]

Calendars

The most elaborate Semitic Calendar which we possess is a very late one, the Harranian. Of this we have two forms, Fihrist (c. 988 AD) and Bērūnī (died 1048 AD) in the following century.[6] Both are imperfect and not always consistent with one another. They represent the latest form of Semitic heathenism, in which the astral elements predominated and Greek theosophy had been combined in some measure with Babylonian astrology. Here the multitude of the feasts is largely due (1) to polytheism and (2) to the fusion of various cults. These two causes are in great measure one. Each of the Syrian cities had its patron deity (conceived as a planetary deity—e.g. the great deity of Edessa was the moon, of Carrhae the planet Venus).[7] We know from Jacob of Sarug that up to the beginning of the sixth century each Syrian town had its own special gods—all these are fused in the later calendar.

The same multiplication of feasts in connection with the worship of many deities at one sanctuary appears earlier. In the second Christian century, the great sanctuary of Syria was Hierapolis (Mabbog). No other people, says Lucian, have so many feasts and sacred assemblies (*De Dea Syria*, 10). At Hierapolis the chief deity was Atargatis, but a whole pantheon of gods and goddesses, heroes and heroines, had their statues in the great temple and its courts. Here, as at Mecca, each pilgrim from every quarter found (or brought) his own god and the worship corresponded to this syncretism. The same syncretism appears still earlier in Babylonia and Assyria—gods of conquered cities are transplanted to the capital of the victor.

Though the gods and goddesses of different Semitic cities and cantons differed in name, planetary attributes, etc., there was at bottom a very great sameness in their functions and worship. This sameness appears to have extended to the festal cycle. Possibly some feasts of particular cities had an historical origin and were anniversaries of the founding of a temple or the like. But most of them were connected with the annual

6.   Flügel (ed.), *Kitâb al-Fihrist*, ch. 9, section 1; C.E. Sachau (ed.), *Chronologie orientalischer Völker von Albêrûnî* (Leipzig: F.A. Brockhaus, 1878), pp. 318-24 = C.E. Sachau (ed.), *The chronology of ancient nations. An English version of the Arabic text of the Athâr-ul-bâkiya of Albîrûnî* (London: W.H. Allen, 1879), pp. 314-20.

7.   M. L'Abbé Martin, 'Discours de Jacques de Saroug sur la chute des idoles', *ZDMG* 29 (1875), p. 110 (Syriac text) = pp. 131-32 (German translation).

recurrence of natural seasons, i.e. they were fixed either by celestial phenomena (as the equinoxes and solstices) or by the agricultural seasons (harvest vintage, etc.), which depend on the motion of the sun in heaven.

Ultimately, among all the civilized Semites the calendar was fixed astronomically with more or less exactness. In Gen. 1.14 the sun and moon are created not only to give light but to serve 'for signs and for seasons and for days' (*l^e'ōtōt ûl^{e}mô$^{'a}$dîm ûl^{e}yāmîm*). The moon gave the month—lunar months of $29\frac{1}{2}$ days among the Hebrews and Harranians. (The Phoenicians perhaps had Egyptian months of 30 days with five epagomens.[8]) This gives a year of $6 \times 59 = 354$ days, so that seven intercalated months are needed in 19 years to keep the rule that Passover falls on the full moon after the vernal equinox. The Passover month is (in the sacred year) the first. The feast of Tabernacles is on the full moon of the seventh month. Thus we have a sacred season at the beginning of the winter half year and the summer half year.

Note also the two ways of reckoning: *Rō'š haššānâ* (New year's day) = the day of trumpet blowing (Lev. 23.24) is 1 Tishri, i.e. the beginning of the 'civil' year. But in the sacred year, Nisan is the first month and Tishri the seventh. Both these ways of reckoning appear among the other Semites. The reckoning from Nisan, i.e. from the equinoctial new moon, is Babylonian. Tishri II = Marcheshwan = Arakh Shamnu = 'eighth month'. It came into use after the Exile (or after Ahaz) with the Babylonian-Syrian names. We find it also in the (North) Arabian calendar of the Hemerologia. On the other hand, the calendars of the Syro-Macedonian cities all begin in autumn (and the Seleucid era is in autumn, 312 BC), simply because the Syrian year ran from autumn to autumn. So too, the Meccan calendar (which with its intercalations was borrowed from the Roman empire) begins in autumn.

Among the Hebrews, as we have seen, each semester begins with a feast. And of this there are traces elsewhere. The first of these is the Passover, which we have seen to be a pre-agricultural feast. The second is the feast of Tabernacles, which is essentially agricultural, as is evident from Exod. 23.16: 'the feast of ingathering, at the outgoing of the year, when thou hast gathered in thy produce from the field'. It is therefore especially a vintage feast. Again, at Baalbek, the month Hag is Tishri I, so that there the winter semester begins with a great feast. The

---

8. Cf. A. Dillmann, 'Über das Kalenderwesen der Israeliten vor dem babylonischen Exil', in *Monatsberichte der königlichen preussischen Akademie der Wissenschaften zu Berlin 1881* (1882), pp. 928-31.

Harranians also had a feast at the full moon of Tishri I.

I now pass on to prove that this astronomical fixing of the feasts is not original. In the oldest Hebrew laws the feast of Tabernacles is essentially an agricultural feast: 'for seven days after thou hast gathered in [the fruits of the earth] from thy threshing floor and wine vat' (Deut. 16.13; cf. Exod. 23.16, 34.22). It is rather a thanksgiving for the old year than a preparation for the new. Above all it is a vintage feast. It may be compared to the Canaanite festival (*hillûlîm*) after the grapes are gathered and trod (Judg. 9.27), and again the feast in the vineyards at Shiloh (Judg. 21.19). We can explain the tabernacles by referring to Hebronite custom, and also by the taboo on entering houses (in Arabia, Hierapolis, Antioch, this is confined to priests). Lev. 23.42 prescribes booths. The feast was first observed in Jerusalem under Nehemiah.[9]

Hag at Helopolis is the name of Tishri (which, with shifting of the date, begins on 22 November). The Harranians also had a feast at the full moon of this month. Note also that at Heliopolis the feast corresponding to Tabernacles is the feast of the year. So it seems to have been in Canaan. In Israel under the judges and kings the Passover was doubtless observed, but it has not at all the same prominence as the autumn feast. It took place 'at the turning of the year' (*t^eqûpat haššānâ*, Exod. 34.22) and we read of dances in the vineyard at the feast in Judg. 21.19. Jeroboam's feast was in the eighth month (of the sacred year). This feast was held at Jerusalem (opening of temple in Ethanim, 1 Kgs 8.2; cf. the feast of *hillûlîm* at Shechem after treading grapes, Judg. 9.27).[10]

This goes with the fact that the year of Canaan and Syria began in autumn. Compare Jerome on Ezek. 1.3: *Apud Orientales populos post collectionem frugum, et torcularia, quando decimae deferebantur in templum, October erat primus mensis*, 'For among eastern peoples after the gathering of the fruits and wine/oil presses, when the tithes were brought into the temple, October was the first month.' Even in P (Lev. 23.24) 1 Tishri is the day of trumpet blowing, i.e. the New Year.

The oldest laws do not date the two feasts *Maṣṣot* (= Passover) and *'Asîp* (= *Sukkôt*).[11] In Deut. 16.1 the Passover is fixed to the month

---

9. Cf. W.R. Smith, 'Tabernacles, feast of', in *Encyclopaedia Britannica* XXIII (Edinburgh: A. & C. Black, 9th edn, 1888), p. 6.

10. Perhaps also the feast at Ramah after which Samuel anointed Saul. For from 1 Sam. 10 it seems that religious services were going on all round; and soon after Saul seems to have been ploughing when he got news of the attack of Jabesh-Gilead.

11. With regard to the name *Sukkôt*, 'Tabernacles', note the allusion to dwelling

Abib, 'Observe the month of Abib' (*šāmôr 'et ḥōdeš hā'ābîb*), almost in such a way as to suggest that the month had a sacred character. Similarly, in the oldest law, Asiph is only 'at the outgoing of the year' (Exod. 23.16, 34.22). In 1 Kgs 8.2 the *ḥag* is simply in the month Ethanim. An exact date could not be conveniently introduced so long as the latter feast was exclusively agricultural, but became necessary when the feast was frequented by distant pilgrims.[12]

New Moon Feasts

These date from ancient times in Israel and resembled the Sabbath, according to 2 Kgs 4.23 and Amos 8.5. From the case of Saul and David one would judge that the feast lasted (or might last) two days (1 Sam. 20.5, 34). Also, in Judith there are two days at New Moon on which fasting is forbidden (Jdt. 8.2). It is plainly not a melancholy occasion, for Saul has a feast and it is credible that the Bethlemite feast was on that day. The conjunction and opposition of the moon were two of the four monthly feasts of the Harranians.

The origin of the observance of the New Moon has been traced to moon worship, which, however, is hardly generally Semitic. With the failure of Lagarde's explanation of *hll, tahlîl*,[13] there remains no clear evidence of moon worship among the ancient Arabs, unless indeed such an inference may be drawn from the use of moonlike amulets, for example, the *śaḥᵃrōnîm* worn by camels among the Midianites and by

in 'tents' (*'ohᵒlîm*), as in the days of an appointed festival (*mô'ēd*, Hos. 12.10, ET 9), but the custom as according to Lev. 23 was new in Nehemiah's time and it was therefore apparently new to do it in Jerusalem. Before this the booths were probably in the vineyards or on the threshing floor (Hos. 9.1); cf. Isa. 1.8 and Hebronite custom. Also the usage during consecration was not to enter house, cf. Arabs, Hierapolis Antioch (priest only). Women *ṣōbᵉ'ôt* were at the door of the Tabernacle (1 Sam. 2.22).

12. In its character Asiph has all the marks of an agricultural merrymaking, as we see from the dances in the vineyards and the booths. Cf. Smith, 'Tabernacles, feast of', in *Encyclopaedia Britannica* XXIII (9th edn), p. 6. For the booths, cf. the *episkēnia*, etc., on which see 'Episkenia', in C. Daremberg and E. Saglio (eds.), *Dictionnaire des antiquités grecques et romaines* II (Paris: Hachette, 1892), p. 698. Note further Dionysiac elements, *thyrsi*, etc., on which see J. Spencer, *De Legibus Hebraeorum Ritualibus* II, Lib. IV, Cap. V (Cambridge: Typis Academicis, 1727), p. 1113. Note especially that it struck Greeks like Plutarch as Bacchic (Plutarch, *Symposiaca*, 4.Q.5).

13. P.A.H. de Lagarde, *Orientalia* II (Göttingen: Dieterich, 1880), p. 19.

women in the time of Isaiah (Isa. 3.18). Among the Hebrews also the observance of the New Moon appears long before we have any clear trace of moon-worship. The latter is attested for Babylonia (the Moon-God Sin), and the moon appears in the long list of Carthaginian divinities in Hannibal's oath, but not in a very prominent position (Polybius, 7.9). That either Ishtar or Astarte was the moon in ancient times is more than doubtful. As regards its observance in old Israel, the new moon is quite like the Sabbath, that is, a day of suspension of work and of gladness and feasting. That it was an *apophras*, a *dies nefaustus*, has been conjectured on general analogies, but there is nothing to confirm this; it were indeed equally plausible to affirm, as some do, that the return of the moon was welcomed with joy. But here also the argument is weak; all religious occasions, or almost all, take a joyous shape in Israel, and perhaps we cannot go further than to say that the Hebrews divided time by months and weeks and thought it fit to close or begin each period by a day of religious observance. This will not be the whole account of the matter, but I do not see any clear path leading us further, for the following reasons:

(a) The agricultural seasons vary from place to place, according to climate. For example, in the Philistine plain, wheat harvest begins about the middle of May or a week later, while at Hebron the first wheat is not cut till about the beginning of June. The variations between more distant parts of the Semitic field were naturally still greater.

(b) Agricultural feasts, i.e. harvest and vintage feasts, would originally, like our harvest homes or harvest thanksgivings, have no fixed date by the calendar, but would take place when the harvest or the vintage was completed. But in this case each township would have to hold the feast itself. A feast to which a large circle of worshippers was gathered from a distance needed to have a *fixed* date by the calendar: for example, Passover and Tabernacles were at the full moon of the first and seventh months respectively. All the ancient Semitic calendars were very imperfect. The months seem generally to have been lunar, though it is possible, as Dillmann argues,[14] that the Phoenicians used the Egyptian month of 30 days. In any case, to keep the months fixed to the seasons was only possible by intercalation, and this, in the infancy of science, was very imperfectly and irregularly done, so that the feasts began to move away from their original season.

In a purely agricultural society, these variations might be kept within

14. See above n. 8.

limit by simply intercalating a month before the harvest month if necessary (so the Hebrews?). But in process of time the great feasts were at the great cities and ceased to be in immediate touch with agriculture. Indeed, in many cases they became more connected with commerce, i.e. fairs. At all events we know as a fact that the calendars did vary immensely. For example, Tammuz, originally the month beginning with the summer solstice, began in the calendar of Heliopolis on 23 August, and at Sidon it corresponded with September.

Sabbath

On the other hand, it can be shown with tolerable certainty that the week is simply a division of the month, and that the Sabbath is not, as Lagarde conjectures, a day sacred to Saturn, but merely the day that seals the weekly period.

The following points should be noted: (1) The way in which the Sabbath was observed—see the difference between the old Sabbath and the rabbinical Sabbath. (2) The association of Sabbath with creation was not there from the beginning. (3) The origin of the week. The Babylonian astrological week was not the origin, since the Sabbath and sacredness of the number seven are older than 24 hours.

A week based on phases of the moon would give 1, 8, 15, 22, 29. If there were two days at New Moon (i.e. a Sabbath + a New Moon) there would be only one week of eight days in two months.

How far was there anything like a Sabbath among other Semites? No Sabbath was connected with the later astrological week. Even at Babylon and in Assyria the astrological week did not prevail in civil life. This appears from the calendars, and also from the fact that the Hebrews in exile seized on the Sabbath and developed it as a mark of their separation.

In a Syllabary, we find Sabattuv = a day of rest of the heart, which proves too much. In a calendar for Elul II, the 7th, 14th, 19th, 21st and 28th have a peculiar character, and certain acts are forbidden on them to kings and others. But these days seem to be unlucky—at least they are not 'days of rest of the heart'. If they are Assyrian Sabbaths they are the exact opposite of the old Hebrew joyous Sabbath. Etymologically, *Shabbāth* may mean 'divider'.

The Hebrew Sabbath could hardly have been developed in a polytheistic society. Its meaning is to consecrate the smaller as well as the larger divisions of time by a religious observance and worship, and in this sense it has shown itself worthy to survive Judaism.

Harvest Feast

Among the Hebrews the proper harvest feast is Pentecost. In Exod. 23.16 it is called 'the feast of harvest' (*ḥag haqqāṣîr*), further defined as 'the firstfruits (*bikkûrîm*) of thy produce which thou sowest in the field', and is accompanied by a gift of firstfruits.[15] In Exod. 34.22 it is 'the feast of weeks, of the firstfruits of wheat harvest' (*ḥag šābuʿōt...bikkûrê qᵉṣîr ḥittîm*). The meaning of this express mention of wheat harvest seems to be that already at this time there was a separate offering of a barley sheaf. That this was the Jewish practice is attested by Josephus and Philo, and is presumably a correct interpretation of Lev. 23.9 *et al.*, in which a sheaf is brought as firstfruits (*rēʾšît*) to the priest on a Sunday at the beginning of harvest. Seven weeks after this, again on a Sunday, the firstfruits (*bikkûrîm*) of wheat are offered in the form of leavened cakes of fine flour and the day is as a holy convocation (*miqrâ qōdeš*), cf. Num. 29.6. The identification of the *šabbāt* with 15 Nisan and of this presentation day with 16 Nisan is as old as the LXX text of Leviticus. But it is not express in the law and cannot be as old as Deuteronomy, in which, indeed, there is no holy convocation (*miqrâ qōdeš*) on the day after the Pannyches, but the people may go home. In Deut. 16.9, the seven weeks of harvest are reckoned simply 'from the time thou beginnest to put the sickle to the standing corn' (*mēhāḥēl ḥermēš baqqāmâ*). Compare also Jer. 5.24, 'the weeks appointed for the harvest' (*šᵉbuʿôt ḥuqqôt qāṣir*).

It has commonly been supposed that the Passover *qua Maṣṣôt* was from the first a harvest feast, and that the *maṣṣôt* are a hasty preparation of new fruits. But in Exod. 23.18 the *maṣṣôt* are the accompaniment of the *ḥag* sacrifice, and this explanation is ample. *Maṣṣôt* are eaten for seven days and so in Deut. 16.3, 'Thou shalt eat no leavened bread with it' (*lōʾ tōʾkal ʿālāyw ḥamēṣ*) *viz.*, with the paschal sacrifice. The argument for making *Maṣṣôt* a harvest feast melts away, therefore, as soon as we have the right explanation of unleavened bread.

The later custom of offering a barley sheaf on 16 Nisan could only

15. Verse 19 'The first of the firstfruits of thy ground thou shalt bring into the house of the Lord thy God' (*rēšît bikkûrê ʾadmatᵉkā tābîʾ bêt Yhwh ᵉlōhêkā*), or is this already the barley sheaf? Probably it is.

come into usage at a sanctuary to which gifts were brought from the earliest districts of Palestine. Barley is not ripe even in the early district of Ramleh till the middle of April, and at Lydda in the Middle Ages the feast of St George (23 April) marked the *waqt aḏ-ḏar'* 'time of seed-produce'.

Accordingly, a strict astronomical fixing of Nisan was not possible. According to *Gemara, Sanh.* 11.2 intercalation took place: (1) if the equinox would fall on 16 Nisan or later, (2) if there could not be barley ready to cut on 16 Nisan, and (3) in response to certain other causes.

When regulated by Passover, Pentecost fell on 5, 6 or 7 Sivan. But *Midrash Ruth* 49.4 makes the wheat harvest go on until around 15 Tammuz.

If the Nisan feasts of the heathen Semites correspond to *Pesaḥ*, we may with great probablility compare the sacred season of harvest—the 50 days beginning with the presentation of the barley sheaf and ending with Pentecost—with a series of feasts found among the heathen Semites which extend roughly speaking according to variations of the calendar through the latter part of spring and the early summer. Of these I note:

(1) a feast at the very beginning of harvest. We know from Muqadassī[16] that even the Mohammedans in Palestine took note of the feast of St George as marking the time 'of the corn'. Apparently, this means the beginning of harvest in the Shephela, for he calls it *'īd Lūd,* 'the festival of Lydda', and 21 April was *sūq Filisṭīn* 'the fair of Palestine', according to Qazwīnī. The fair would not fall in such a wheat country actually in harvest, but before it. St George, who slew the Dragon at Beirut, is the successor of Heracles, who slew the Hydra, or the Perseus (*pārāš, fāris*) of Tarsus and Joppa. And as the market at Deir Ayyūb is also on 23 Nisan, and is connected with the grave of Job and with a sacred spring which he opened by stamping with his foot (and this at Ashtaroth-Qarnaim and in a region where the fair must have been pastoral and some time before harvest), I see here a feast which became a harvest feast on the Phoenician lowlands but originally corresponded rather to the Passover.

(2) In Iyyar (May, or on the lunar calendar rather April–May) we

16. Muqadassī, *Descriptio imperii Moslemici* (*Aḥsan al-Taqāsīm fī Ma'rifat al-Aqālim*) (ed. M.J. de Goeje; Bibliotheca geographorum Arabicorum 3; Leiden: E.J. Brill, 1877), p. 183. [ET Mukaddasi (ed. G. Le Strange), *Description of Syria including Palestine*; London: Palestine Pilgrim's Text Society, 1886, p. 77].

have a series of important feasts. On 17 Iyyar, there was the Pannychis at Edessa, with dancing, lights, relation of myths, etc. There was feasting for seven days previously.[17] Among the Harranians, 17 Iyyar is the feast of *Bāb at-Tibn*.[18] At Antioch, the anniversary of the Tyche of the city was 22 May. At Antioch, further, the triennial Maiuma are said to have been celebrated in May as a 'theatrical and nocturnal feast' (*skēnikē kai nukterinē heortē*) with lights, etc. This, I fancy, must agree with the feast of the Tyche, when the sacrifice was at sunrise.

At Edessa, the harvest seems to have not been begun as early as 17 May. There is, however, a very curious line of connection to be traced here. In P, the flood begins on 17 Iyyar (Gen. 7.11). According to Berosus, the Babylonian legend makes its date 15 Daesius. Here, Daesius is almost certainly Iyyar. This may at first sight seem mere coincidence. But Bērūnī[19] tells us that the heathen Syrians kept the 17th of each month sacred because of the flood. In Lucian (*De Dea Syria*, 13) there are two annual feasts at Hieropolis in which water from the 'sea' is poured on the floor of the temple and descends into the *chasma* through which the flood disappeared. Melito[20] says the rite was to prevent the demon of the well from rising to destroy men. The feasts are probably spring and autumn. The autumn fair at Mabbog (Hierapolis) in Bērūnī's time was 1 September,[21] which agrees fairly with the water ceremony at Tyre in September, and the pouring out of water from Shiloah (Siloam) at the feast of Tabernacles as a rain charm. If the exact six-months period was observed this would throw the spring feast to 1 Nisan. But this is doubtless the date rather of the great festival of the lamp (*lampas*) or fire (*purē*), which Lucian seems to distinguish from the two rites observed by the sea (*es thalassan*). I apprehend, therefore, that the spring water-rite (of which the agricultural meaning is indubitable) was, like Pentecost, less than six months from the other. Whether it was actually on 15–17 Iyyar may be hard to say.

17. W. Wright (ed.), *The Chronicle of Joshua the Stylite* (Cambridge: Cambridge University Press, 1882), pp. 27 and 30.

18. So Bērūnī. See Sachau (ed.), *Chronologie orientalischer Völker von Albêrûnî*, p. 321 = Sachau (ed.), *The chronology of ancient nations*, p. 317.

19. See Bērūnī in Sachau (ed.) *Chronologie orientalischer Völker von Albêrûnî*, p. 321 = Sachau (ed.), *The chronology of ancient nations*, p., 318.

20. Melito, 'Oration', in W. Cureton, *Spicilegium Syriacum* (London: Rivingtons, 1855), p. 45 (= Syriac, p. 25).

21. For Bērūnī, see Sachau (ed.), *Chronologie orientalischer Völker von Albêrûnî*, p. 273 = Sachau (ed.) *The chronology of ancient nations*, p. 265

In Babylonia, the rise of the Euphrates, which fills the fertilizing canals, is in May. That a religious ceremony should be connected with this is natural, and is supported by the analogy of Egypt. And that the flood is not an exaggeration of the autumn rains but of the river-rise is clear from the fountains of the great deep being broken up (in both the Hebrew and the Babylonian account and also in Lucian.)

In P, Noah issues from the ark on 27 Iyyar (Gen. 8.14-16), but as his sacrifice is not in P this hardly means more than that the flood lasted a solar year. Both in J (Gen. 7.4) and in the Babylonian account there are seven days' preparation, which would agree with the week of feasting before 17 Iyyar. In the Babylonian account the flood lasts but 14 days, so that if the feast of the 17th is really the beginning of the flood, the feast at the exit would be at the New Moon. But it seems quite possible that the two-day Harranian feast on 1 and 2 Iyyar represents the beginning, that the feast of the 17th corresponds to Noah's sacrifice, and that in P, this correspondence is disguised by the desire to make a solar year of it. For in P there are 150 days till the Ark rests (Gen. 8.3-4), and this is just the five months that would be from 1 and 2 Iyyar to the fair of 1 September at Mabbog (Hierapolis).

PRIESTS AND THE PRIESTLY ORACLE

If I am called upon to begin what I have to say on the subject of priests with a definition, I do not know that I can in a few words come nearer the matter than by saying that a priest is a sacred minister, whose stated business is to perform on behalf of the community certain public ritual acts, especially sacrifices. Such ministers are found in connection with all the great religions of antiquity and can indeed hardly be dispensed with where the regular maintenance of the traditional functions of religion is regarded as a necessary part of social order.

In antiquity, as we saw at length in the first course of lectures, the gods are part of the social community—the clan or the state—and their relations with men are conceived as regulated by fixed principles, and are to be maintained in integrity, to the advantage and welfare of the community by the sedulous observance of certain traditional rules of conduct, especially of traditional forms of worship, which are regulated by precedents handed down from generation to generation. To a certain extent every member of the community has religious duties, for the performance of which he is responsible to the public as well as to his own conscience; for if any member of the society offends the gods by impious acts or by impious neglect, his offence is dangerous not merely to himself but to the whole community, and may bring wrath on all his neighbours unless it is duly punished or expiated. Of this feeling there are sufficient examples even in the Old Testament.[1] To a certain extent, therefore, the maintenance of the communal religion in its integrity depends on the individual actions of every member, the community through its official organs merely watching over individuals and seeing that they do not with impunity imperil their neighbours by conduct grossly impious.

But we have also seen, in speaking of sacrifices, that the most

---

1. Cf. Achan (Josh. 7) and Jonathan and the honey (1 Sam. 14.24-30).

important functions of ancient religion were not performed by individuals in their private capacity, but were the joint act of the whole community. The oldest sacrifices were acts of communion in which all the members of a clan participated, and even when private sacrifices became common they were generally offered on public occasions, at the stated festal seasons, and thus formed part of a communal act of worship which called for some measure of direction and organization on the part of constituted authorities. However, at Shiloh every man seems independent, and we do not readily see what was the function of the priest unless perhaps the burning of the fat (1 Sam. 2.12-17). But even in Arabia, where each worshipper or group brings its own offering, there is at least the *wuqūf*, which is terminated by a sign, so that there is some organization. Still more was the presidence of a constituted authority acting on behalf of the congregation necessary where the sacrifice as well as the feast had a public communal character, e.g. in the sacrifices which were offered at the beginning and close of a campaign, at the accession of a king, at the sealing of a treaty, or in periodical atoning ceremonies. On such occasions sacrifices of an official kind, on behalf of the whole community of worshippers, were offered not only by the Hebrews but by the Arabs, among whom religion had less of formal organization than among any other Semitic people, and most of its exercises were left, to a most unusual extent, to the mere initiative of individuals.

On the whole, then, it would seem that, from the remotest times, the right discharge of the prescribed acts of communal worship involved some form, however elementary, of religious organization and sacred ministry. Public acts, which to be effective, i.e. acceptable to the gods, required to be performed with due attention to rule and precedent, were necessarily conducted and led by some responsible representative of the worshipping community, and in this representative function the germ was already contained out of which a stated priesthood could not fail to grow, as soon as the ceremonies of religion became at all copious and elaborate.

It must, however, be noted that there is a long step from the recognition of priestly functions to the institution of a separate priestly order. Where ceremonial is simple and the tradition regulating it devoid of complexity, the civil heads of the community—the elders or the king—may naturally act as representatives and leaders of the people in matters of worship as in other public ceremonies. In ancient Greece and Rome the king was the acting head of the state religion and when the regal power came to an end his sacred functions were not transferred to the ordinary priests, but either they were distributed among high officers of state or the title of king was still preserved as that of a sacred functionary, as in the case of the *rex sacrorum* at Rome and the *archōn basileus* at Athens.

Similarly among the Semites. In Nilus's sacrifice,[2] the leader of the procession and the hymn who strikes the victim and drinks the first blood is 'anyone...either of the rulers or of the priests, venerable in age and hoariness' (*tis...ē tōn basileuontōn ē tōn hēlikiai kai gērai semnunomenōn hiereōn*—where nothing more seems to lie in the title 'priest' than the venerable age which marks out an elder of the tribe as fit to preside in the sacred ceremony. Among the Arabs, where there was a temple there was a regularly constituted keeper of the house and treasure of the god, but such formal priesthoods, where they existed, had seemingly little or nothing to do with sacrifice. The man who presented a private offering killed his own victim and seemingly performed the whole ritual himself. In a communal sacrifice, in like manner, it was simply a chief or elder who was chosen to conduct the sacred rites.

Similarly among the Hebrews in old times. The rule which prohibits the laity from access to the altar has no place in the oldest legislation. Exod. 20.22-26, the law of the altar, was spoken to the people (not to the priests) and specially to the laity. Historical examples of private sacrifice are those of Gideon (Judg. 6.26, 28) and Manoah (Judg. 13.15-20).

Examples of public sacrifice include those by Saul (1 Sam. 13.9) and David (2 Sam. 6.17). Solomon (1 Kgs 9.25) sacrificed in person. These examples are after a priesthood existed at Shiloh and elsewhere. Jeroboam stands by the altar to burn incense (1 Kgs 13.1)—not, we may be sure, against use and wont. Again, David's sons are priests (2 Sam. 8.18), though David had Abiathar and Zadok, an institution which may be compared with the Tyrian custom of choosing the chief priests from the royal family.[3]

But though the Hebrew kings, in virtue of their representative function, took the first part in public religious ceremonies, they were not

---

2.   St Nilus, *Narratio* III, in J.-P. Migne, *Patrologiae cursus completus. Series Graeca* LXXIX (Paris: J.-P. Migne, 1865), col. 613A.

3.   Perhaps it was on David's part a solitary experiment in imitation of Tyre. But if so, it was not continued, though the kings sacrificed when they pleased down to the time of the Captivity, e.g. Ahaz, 2 Kgs 16.12-13. Cf. Jer. 30.21.

consecrated priests and there is no sign that they sought to combine in their persons two separate dignities, kingly and priestly, as was the case in Egypt. The kingship was a sacred office, for it was god-given, but its sanctity was not derived from the possession of ritual privileges and was not enhanced by the performance of sacred functions. The usual talk about the 'oriental theocracies' meaning 'priestly sovereignties' has no application to ancient Israel. The origin of priest-kingship among the Semites is much more modern and falls to be explained at the end, not at the beginning of our history of the priesthood.

The formation of separate priesthoods and of a privileged priestly office was due to the co-operation of a number of causes, which we may now proceed to examine. The priesthood whose history is best known is that of Israel. But it becomes clear only by the aid of critical analysis, and even so there are great gaps in the record. I will not therefore begin with it, but with the Semite country where priesthood was least developed, Arabia. In Arabia we do not find priests at every sacred spot, but only where there is a temple with treasure and equipments and especially an idol (*watan, ṣanam*). The names used for priests show this (*sādin, ḥājib*). The priesthood was hereditary in certain families, whose property the sanctuary was, and this was often a noble family, for it was noble families, we are told, who had idols of their own. In some cases, it was a family foreign to the tribe that held the land, a relic of older inhabitants. Such families had difficulties in maintaining their privilege. For the idol *Yaghūth* there was a battle. Of course, at a sanctuary like Mecca the family which has the ministry of the temple (*sidānah*) ceases to be strictly proprietor. But the hereditary custodianship is a sort of freehold, which brings not inconsiderable fees: (1) from the oracle; (2) from hiring out clothes for persons worshipping or consulting the oracle—priestly clothes;[4] and (3) perquisites.[5]

---

4.   Can *'erkô* in 2 Kgs 12.5 (ET 4) be *'rk* in the sense of a suit of clothes? If so, the text is corrupt, and indeed LXX seems to show this. One might conjecture *kesep 'îš 'ōbēd ḥassap*. Then for *napšôt* we seem to have, besides *psuchōn, psēphō* and *labōn*. This, however, is fanciful and *labōn* is probably an insertion *ad sensum*. Then *napšôt* will be a gloss on *'erkô* and *'ōbēr* for *'ōbēd* a correction to make the passage agree (as the Chronicler takes it) with Exod. 30.12-16. Then *kesep 'ōbēd 'îs kesep 'erkô* will be 'the money paid by worshippers, every one for his suit', in which he is allowed to enter the *naos*, for the collection is taken at the door of the *naos*, not of the court.

5.   Hereditary priesthoods also existed in Phoenicia. At Paphos there were Cinyradae, whose ancestor was Cinyras, father of Adonis and of daughters who

Here, then, the priest is primarily a man of the family that owns the sanctuary, who is set apart as custodian of the family property. And he acquires a further priestly importance when the sanctuary is visited or oracles are consulted by people who have no rights in the sanctuary. When we find a priestly family staying on at the sanctuary when all their fellow tribesmen have moved away, we see that in Arabia the profits of the sanctuary from outsiders (combined with the security of its asylum) were enough to outweigh the tribal ties; and on the other hand that the newcomers, while they were glad to use the sanctuary, did not venture to remove the priests. *Why*, we see from the Assyrian emigrants into Israel, who asked for Hebrew priests (2 Kgs 17.24-28). We may compare the general rules, which are certainly old, as to the danger of approaching holy places, e.g. the fence at Sinai (Exod. 19.23).

There is a parallel in old Israel in the story of Micah (Judg. 17–18): (1) a private sanctuary is in the charge of a son; (2) a Levite is a better priest, doubtless because the Levite knew better the ritual and tradition; (3) the *sacra* pass into the hands of the Danites, who take the priest with them and his office continues hereditary until the Captivity. Here we have the fixed priesthood based as in Arabia on two things: (1) custody of costly *sacra*; (2) the tradition of their safe use, especially in the oracle, of which more presently.[6] Thus at Nob, Ahimelech[7] has under his charge the 'ephod', with which he flees, and votive gifts such as Goliath's sword (1 Sam. 21.9; 23.6). In the Canaanite temple at Shechem there was money (Judg. 9.4), which was at the disposal of the townsmen, but must have had a custodian. Teraphim and ephod, according to Hos. 3.4, were a necessary part of the equipment of every shrine in Ephraim and these, we know, were means of divination. In old Israel the judgment of God at the sanctuary is the ultimate appeal to which all hard cases were referred

leaped into the sea and became alcyones, so appointing himself divine. Sometimes the priesthoods are *foreign*, as in Arabia. R. Pietschmann, *Geschichte der Phönizier* (Berlin: G. Grote, 1889), p. 221, cites the Tamyradae at Paphos, said to be Cilicians. J. Wellhausen, *Prolegomena zur Geschichte Israels* (Berlin: G. Reimer, 1883), pp. 153-54, n. 2 [ET *Prolegomena to the History of Israel* (Edinburgh: A. & C. Black, 1885), pp. 147-48, n. 3], supposes that some of the Hebrew Levites were Canaanite, which is very likely. Many Levites were certainly foreigners.

6.   Also the ordeal (*qasāma, nār al-hūla*), cf. Deut. 21.1-9 and also the water of jealousy (Num. 5.11-31).

7.   [WRS mistakenly wrote 'Abiathar' for 'Ahimelech'—'Ahimelech has under his charge the "ephod" with which he flees.' I have reworded to make it correct.— J.D.]

(1 Sam. 2.25; Exod. 21.6; 22.8-9); *'elōhîm* do not equal judges but God and the oracle of the priest is of more weight than the word of the diviner. David drops Gad for Abiathar and his ephod (cf. 1 Sam. 22.5, 20-23; 23.6). In the public sanctuaries also (of which Dan was one of the most important) the priest is primarily custodian of the sanctuary and its treasures, and its oracle.

We are apt to think, in accordance with the Levitical legislation, that the divine oracle is necessarily the Urim and Thummim of the Aaronite High Priest. The sanctuary of Dan (Judg. 18.17-20) and the passage of Hos. 3.4 prove that this was not so and still more the account of Levi in Deut. 33.8-11 (northern). But from the time of Moses the Tabernacle and the Ark were the great seat of God's decisions, and its ministers were from Moses, the priest of this sanctuary, the priests of the house of Eli, and the northern priests generally (for Moses is the faithful one whom Jehovah tried at Massa and whose cause he asserted at Meribah, Deut. 33.8). Let us therefore look at this sanctuary more exactly and see how it resembles and how it differs from other priestly sanctuaries of the Semites.

The original Tabernacle was a simple tent outside camp,[8] where Moses meets with God and where his aedituus, Joshua, remains when he is away (Exod. 33.7; Num. 12). Unfortunately, the original account of the making of this Tabernacle and its relation to the Ark is not given. In E it is the sign of divine presence which God allows to Israel when they are forbidden, for the offence of the golden calf, to remain at Sinai. At the same time it is in God's grace the true answer to the people's demand to Aaron, 'make us gods, who shall go before us' (Exod. 32.1). It does not contain an idol; Jehovah appears in it in the pillar of fire, but it continued something which, when the pillar of fire ceased, was still regarded as securing the divine presence. This is clear from the history of the Ark, especially of its wanderings from Shiloh to Beth-Shemesh, Kiriath-Jearim, and Jerusalem (1 Sam. 4.1–7.2; 2 Sam. 6), and David's words at the revolt of Absalom (2 Sam. 15.24-26). In the old narrative the Tabernacle and Ark are never mentioned together. The Tabernacle is the place of oracles, but when the camp moves we hear not of the Tabernacle but of the Ark. The Ark, it seems, has no significance except as the box in which the apparatus of the Tabernacle is carried. What was originally in the Ark we do not learn from the original narrative.

8.   Contrast the Priestly Tabernacle in the camp, which resembles the post-exilic temple.

According to later accounts, it contained the Law, either Deuteronomy (Deut. 31.25) or the Decalogue and nothing more.[9] The very name, 'Ark of God's testimony (or Law)' (*'arôn hā'ēdût*) has been shown to belong only to late authors. The old name is 'Ark of the Lord'. But these statements, varying as they do in detail, yet point to a truth. The Ark and its sanctuary was the seat of Torah (divine decision), not originally written but oral. And this would indicate that in the Ark were carried the apparatus of the priestly oracle. What this was we cannot tell. Was it perhaps after all an ephod, such as we find at every sanctuary later? Was this made of the ornaments put off by the people in Exod. 33.6? In the mutilated state of the sources we cannot say. Certainly at this time the presence of Jehovah was not 'between the cherubim'.

It may seem that Num. 12.8 and Exod. 33.11 are against this. But a little thought will satisfy us that the account of Moses' revelation there given is not literal but idealized. God speaks to Moses 'mouth to mouth as a man with his friend' (Exod. 33.11; cf. Num. 12.8). Literally this is impossible, for 'no man hath seen God at any time' (John 1.18; cf. Exod. 33.20). It appears in Numbers 12 that the essential point is the distinction between Moses and the prophets, who receive an inner revelation by (subjective) vision and dream. This objective character belongs to an oracle and, as we have seen in David's history, made the priestly revelation preferred to that through a seer. And with this agree not only Deut. 33.8, where the Urim and Thummim are given to Moses, but also the oldest account in Exod. 18.19, where Moses brings the people's causes 'to God', the phrase used later of appeal to the priestly oracle. I apprehend, therefore, that the later oracle is based on that of the Ark and Tabernacle, and if an ephod or image is added, that takes the place of the visible pillar of cloud before which the oracle was sought.

Here the question arises how far the appurtenances and methods of the priestly lot in Israel agree with those of other Semites. We may note also the evidence for divination in small portable tabernacles. We learn of portable shrines of the Phoenicians in Diodorus Siculus, 20.14.3 and of woven *bāttîm* 'houses' for the Asherah in 2 Kgs 23.7. Macrobius, *Saturnalia* 1.23.13 declares, *Vehitur enim similacrum dei Heliopolitani ferculo*, 'For the statue of the god of Heliopolis is borne in a litter.' Amos 5.26 is correctly rendered 'tabernacle of your King'. Note especially the evidence of Servius (in his commentary on Virgil's

---

9.   1 Kgs 8.9 is a passage which we do not possess in its original shape.

Aeneid, 6.68) and Syriac glosses[10] for oracles from the deities in the *prakk* or on litters. Further, with Spencer,[11] we should note the close parallel between the carrying of the Ark in a new cart in connection with the Philistines and David (1 Sam. 6.7; 2 Sam. 6.3) and the Phoenician worship of Agrotes with his 'very venerable image, and a shrine drawn by a pair of beasts'.[12]

The sacred oracle lasts and finally passes into the (obsolete) Urim and Thummim of the High Priest. But gradually, instead of new appeals to the oracle, precedent is quoted, going back to Moses (cf. Deut. 17.11).

The following were the causes that made priestly mediation at the sanctuary necessary: (1) from the earliest times taboos and strict rules, which every man could not conveniently observe; (2) the increasing complexity of ritual; (3) still more, the growth of sanctity of certain holy things, which not everyone can dare to touch.

10. E.g. J.G.E. Hoffmann, *Opuscula Nestoriana* (Kiel: G. von Maack; Paris: Maisonneuve, 1880), p. 115, line 15.

11. Spencer, *De Legibus Hebraeorum Ritualibus*, II, p. 838 (Lib. III, Diss. V, Cap. I, Sect. VI).

12. Philo of Byblos, in Eusebius, *Praep. Ev.*, 1.10.12. (Oxen, not horses, as in Herodotus 1.31 in connection with Hera.)

PRIESTS (CONTINUED), DIVINERS, PROPHETS

In the last lecture the function of priests was revealed. In old Israel, while other methods of revelation were recognized, the priestly oracle stood first. This function gradually declined in importance, especially after the rise of spiritual prophecy to influence in the state (Elisha). After the Restoration, there were no Urim and Thummim—the priestly Torah was now not revelation, but exposition of sacred Law. And after this was booked and circulated, this function too fell more and more into the hands of the scribes.

The mediatorial function in worship now became prominent and side by side with this the old simple organization of the priesthood as we find it at Shiloh gave way to an elaborate organization of a graduated mass of functionaries.

The development of priestly service was unquestionably largely influenced from Canaan. Solomon took the design of his temple from Tyre, and from the Canaanites and Phoenicians in like manner seems to have been derived the manner of priestly service. We shall offer a brief proof of this. First, with regard to priestly dress, the linen was ultimately from Egypt. Among the Hebrews the dress of ordinary priests consisted of a tunic (according to Josephus *podērēs*, 'reaching the feet', close fitting, sleeved and low-necked), drawers of linen and the *'abnēṭ* or girdle of office, also worn by ministers (cf. Shebna and Eliakim, son of Hilkiah, Isa. 22.21). The limitation to linen is Egyptian and Phoenician, and Phoenician monuments show the *mgb'h* or dome-like cap.[1] Similarly, in Lucian, *De Dea Syria*, 42, the priests are all in white with a cap (*pilos*) on the head. Again, Silius Italicus, *Punica*, 3.24-25 says of the sanctuary at Gades that *all* worshippers before the altar are in white—*velantur corpora lino et Pelusiaco praefulget stamine vertex*, 'linen covers their limbs, and their foreheads are adorned with a head-

---

1. Pietschmann, *Geschichte der Phönizier*, p. 226 n. 1C.

band of Pelusian flax.' This shows that, as in the Baal worship at Samaria (2 Kgs 10.22) and in some Arabian sanctuaries, a priestly dress was required of those who entered the temple. Women, according to Silius Italicus, *Punica*, 3.21-22, did not enter. So among the Jews they did not pass beyond their own court. When all worshippers are so dressed the priests require a distinction. In Silius Italicus the *sacrifica vestis* 'garment of sacrifice' has a *latus clavus* 'broad stripe' (*Punica*, 3.27), which also appears as the mark of the priestly dress in Herodian (*History*, 5.5.10) and is attested in Palmyrene monuments. The ordinary priest's garment in Hebrew has purple and other colours only on the embroidery of the belt, of which, however, the ends were knotted and hung down to the ankles like a scarf or (when it would hinder work) thrown back over the shoulder.

Another point of resemblance concerns the priests officiating *pes nudus* 'bare foot'. This is attested at Gades (Silius Italicus, *Punica*, 3.28) and similarly among the Hebrew priests, according to a tradition which is doubtless sound. Indeed, the Talmud says that no one might wear shoes in the temple (*b. Yeb.* 6*b*). The alternative was linen stockings (Herodian, *History*, 5.5.10) as in Egypt priests wear only sandals of papyrus (Herodotus, 2.37). In Silius Italicus, *Punica*, 3.26, the cap goes with 'heads shaven' (*tonsae comae*), which again agrees with Ezek. 44.20. Doubtless the hair had to be covered with the cap.

One point of difference is that the Hebrew priest is girt, but in Silius Italicus, *Punica*, 3.26, 'it is their custom to offer incense with robes ungirt' (*discinctis mos tura dare*). I cannot explain this. The priestly girdle (*'abnēṭ*) is *hemyān* in Aramaic, which seems to be Persian. The High Priestly dress again is partly the *old* priest's dress modified, a linen ephod (*'ēpôd bad*) and robe (*m͏ᵉ 'îl*) as worn by Samuel, but consists mainly of the princely purple and tiara, though this is not sacrificial and so linen is substituted on the day of Atonement.

In the High Priestly dress, note the bells and pomegranates. Cf. Exod. 28.35: 'And its sound shall be heard when he goes into the holy place before the Lord, and when he comes out, lest he die.'[2]

---

2. Therefore to keep away fatal influences (explained away by Ecclus. 45.9 as a memorial of the people before God). J. Wellhausen, *Reste arabischen Heidentumes* (*Skizzen und Vorarbeiten* III; Berlin: G. Reimer, 1887), p. 144 compares Nab. 17.12, where the noise of metal pendants is used to drive the demons from a fever patient. That they are amulets like the phylactery and so borrowed from heathenism seems certain. Cf. Josephus, *Jewish Wars*, 5.57.

We may compare Lucian of Samosata, *De Dea Syria*, 42, who reports that 'Many priests have been appointed for the inhabitants, some of whom slaughter the sacrificial beasts and some bear the libations. Others are called "Fire-bearers" and others "Altar Attendants". While I was there more than three hundred attended the sacrifice.' (Priests bearing cressets on the end of staves seem also to be shown on Phoenician monuments, doubtless to supply holy fire, perhaps also to cense.)

See also the painted inscription of Citium which has, *inter alia, pōr^{e}kîm* (veil keepers), *šōm^{e}rê hassap* (door keepers), slaughterers (Levites and, still earlier, foreigners), singing women and dancing women like the maidens at Shiloh. (Singing and dancing are attested both of men [cf. David] and women among the Hebrews, but were not apparently a priestly function.) Jewish tradition prescribes dances of grave and dignified persons in the court of women at the feast of Tabernacles. The peculiar dance of the priests of Baal in 1 Kgs 18.26 is a sort of limp, presumably curtseying. Heliodorus (*Aethiopica*, 4.16-17), describes a festal dance of Tyrians in honour of Melqart with spinning like the dancing dervishes and variations of swift leaps and gliding motion. We may compare the name of the deity, *Ba'al Marqōd* (Baal of the dance) and the orgiastic dance of the Galli, mentioned in Lucian, *De Dea Syria*, 50. The dance is the usual expression of gladness, but in these forms is doubtless (as in an Islamic *dikr*) an artificial means of excitement. Perhaps we should compare the soaring, posturing, standing on head, etc., at the tombs of Obadiah, Elisha, and John the Baptist at Samaria. At Hierapolis there are besides the proper priests a multitude of flute players, etc., and of frenzied and insane women. For it was the custom of these shrines to gather round them troops of half-insane men and women who worked themselves into frenzies ascribed to divine influence. Similar traces of wild enthusiasm appear in early Israel (cf. Saul among the prophets, 1 Sam. 10.10-12, 19.20-24). But characteristic is the discouragement of mere frenzy. The prophetic inspiration is sane and self-possessed. The Phoenician inspired maniacs are under priestly control—similarly at the temple—but the prophets emancipate themselves.

Among the Hebrews, as among other nations, the sacred lot at the sanctuary was not the only means of revelation. The means of consulting the divine will among the Semites are very numerous and of these some are condemned in the Bible as altogether heathenish, others are permitted if not conducted in a heathenish way, but 'in the name of Jehovah'. The *permitted methods* are often summed up under the name 'prophecy', which term is used to cover revelation by dream and vision, as well as the more developed spiritual prophecy in which visions play a very subordinate part, and dreams hardly occur at all.

The *forbidden arts* again, of which a full enumeration is given in Deut. 18.10-11, may be broadly divided into two heads: (1) pure divination; (2) black art, magic or divination with a magical element involving the use of charms and material means to constrain the gods or ghosts and spirits. The functions of the former present a great similarity to the *legitimate* oracle, and the functions of the seers in early Israel; they are illegitimate, mainly as associated with the worship of other gods. Magical arts, on the other hand, were forbidden in well-regulated heathen states, as in Greece, and in Israel we find Saul putting them down at a time when there was not yet the broad difference that existed between the heathen *mantis* and the Hebrew seer or prophet. To this class of prac- tisers of black art are to be reckoned in Deut. 18.10-11 what the English version gives as 'a witch, or a charmer, or a consulter with familiar spirits, or a wizard, or a necromancer' (more exactly the last two are a wizard who conjures by magical drugs and material charms, or by words of incantation, or one who consults with subterranean spirits [*'ôb*] or with a familiar spirit (*yidde'ōnî*) or with ghosts).

Each of these may be briefly illustrated. The use of 'medicines' and 'incantations' to constrain supernatural influences (to give information or other assistance) is general among all savage peoples. Of the latter, the commonest form among the Hebrews seems to have been serpent charming, which now in the East is a mere trick, but probably was originally connected with the great reverence paid to snakes, especially as revealers.

Of the material means of enchantment (magic brews and the like) used in Bible times we have little information. They were particularly current in Babylon. To this head may be reckoned amulets against the evil eye and the many charms (bones, dried heads, etc.) which seem to have been originally derived from sacrifice.

Very prominent among the heathen-minded in Israel was the appeal to ghosts and familiar spirits. With regard to the Witch of Endor, the ghost was not *seen* by the consulter and the method of consulting the *'ôb* (Syriac *zakkûrê*) was ventriloquism, the voice coming from the ground, or from the belly of the sorcerer. The *ra'î* or *tābi'* of the Arabs = *yidde'ōnî* of Hebrew.

Methods of pure divination are: (1) *qesem*—this is in Aramaic a general word including all forms of revelation, but primarily it is the oracle derived from *sacra* at the sanctuary—the counterpart of the priestly lot; (2) The m^e '*ōnēn* was perhaps the seer who gives oracles in an inspired recitation (Arabic *saj'*). His function is similar to that of the popular *rō'eh*. The characteristic is a certain amount of frenzy, and this is, in point of form, the main difference from Hebrew prophecy; (3) Augury. This was most developed among the Arabs. The emancipation from slavery to such signs is one of the great practical boons conferred on Israel by its religion.

We are now in a position to estimate the truth of the frequent assertion according to which prophecy is a characteristic product of the Semitic race.

Prophecy and Divination

The great thinkers of the Aryan race are philosophers, we are told; those of the Semitic race, prophets. Those who take this view are, of course, thinking mainly of the Hebrews and the Arabs, and among the Arabs mainly of Mohammed, but also of other leaders within the sphere of Islam, down to the present age, such as Shāmil and 'Abd al-Ḳādir, who have laid claims, more or less distinctly, to a prophetic character. But from the Hebrews and Arabs a generalization is often drawn including the other Semites. Only the other day a reviewer said that it is a mistake to suppose that the Old Testament could only have been produced by the Hebrews.

In point of fact, there is not the smallest historical evidence that anything like Amos, Isaiah, or Jeremiah was produced by any of the heathen Semites, or even that any branch of the Semites rose to a religious condition in which such prophecy would have been possible. It is true that, if we accept the silly definition which some still think orthodox, that prophecy equals prediction, then there was prophecy in all Semitic, nay, in all ancient nations. But the Old Testament, notably in that memorable passage, Deut. 18.9-19, draws a sharp distinction between the true prophet and the diviner and it does not make the difference turn on the truth or falsehood of the predictions. Indeed, all early nations are firmly convinced that their diviners have a fine faculty of seeing the secrets of the past, present and future, and even to this day many people not devoid of intelligence are firmly persuaded of the reality of second sight, etc. If the proof of the unique character of the

Old Testament revelation is to be rested on a comparison between the fulfilled predictions of the Old Testament and those recorded in the literature of other nations, the victory of the Bible will not be very decisive.

The Bible itself, I say, does not rest the argument on this. Even in Isa. 41.22, where the idols are challenged 'to show the beginnings, what they are that we may consider them, and know the issues of them, or to announce things to come', the sense of the challenge is defined by the context and the following 'Do good or evil.' It is not merely to *predict* that the idols are challenged, but to produce an effect in history such as Jehovah produces, and to announce it beforehand as their work. In Deut. 13.1-3 the prophet or dreamer of dreams, who gives a sign that is fulfilled as an inducement to idolatry, is not to be listened to, but is to be slain. It is not denied that the idolatrous sign may come true; but if so, Jehovah is trying (*m^{e}nasseh*) his people. In Deut. 18.21-22, the man who speaks as a prophet in Jehovah's name is expected to verify his commission by a fulfilled prediction. This is a remains of the old point of view, but is not the essence of spiritual prophecy.

Again, it is also true that if the mark of a prophet is to speak in ecstasy, pouring forth mechanically a revelation in which his reason has no part, prophecy is not confined to Israel, nor to the Semites; for to speak in an ecstasy or frenzy is the mark of the Greek *mantis* as well as of the Syrian *qāṣem* and the Arabic *kāhin*. Where divination is a trade, the ecstasy is not seldom simulated, much oftener it is artificially produced; but it is not open to question that among primitive peoples generally mantic frenzy really occurs and that its utterances are taken as revelations, though often, as in Greece, they require to be interpreted by a *prophētēs*. But it is certain that Amos and Isaiah did not speak mechanically in a frenzy. Of the New Testament prophets, likewise, Paul demands self-control, such as implies that the faculties of reason and judgment are awake (1 Cor. 14.32). The mechanical theory is not biblical, but flows from Philo's half-heathen philosophy of religion.[3]

Those who take a higher view of the prophet than this, and view him as a teacher of religious truths, and that not as a philosopher speaking by reason, but as a man moved by divine inspiration which carries his

---

3. Also in John 11.51, *prophētēs*, is used in the Greek not in the Hebrew sense. In Greek, any instrument through whom the God declares himself is a *prophētēs*. It is a case of *klēdonismos* where the *klēdōn* is accepted in a sense not meant.

reason and utterance with it, and who at the same time take prophecy to be a peculiar product of the Semitic genius, rest mainly on Mohammed.[4]

In fact, Mohammed has absolutely no fresh religious idea. Nor has he any fresh application of religious truth to the present juncture. His political revelations are purely his own private policy. The swoon, which he was able to produce, is merely a cloak in the later Suras for the coldest political judgment or a veil for selfish ambition combined—such are men—with a real zeal against polytheism and real belief in the Judgment. The Meccans thought at first that Mohammed was a *kāhin*, a view he indignantly disclaimed. Musailima and the tribe of other prophets and prophetesses are mere imitators of Mohammed, and the later prophets of Islam are built on the same model. They were mostly *not* Semites or not pure Semites, far oftener Africans and in most cases, like Al-Mutanabbī, the Almohade Mahdī, etc., mere conscious impostors, or heroes like ʿAbd al-Kādir. Like many heroes, they have acquired a sort of superstitious confidence in their own judgment which takes a form determined by the superstition of those around them. Certainly these are not prophets in the Hebrew sense. What approaches nearest to the self-consciousness of the prophets is the mystic inner light of a man like Savonarola or, in later days, of the Persian Bāb. But the discussion of such cases carries us beyond the specific field of Semitic religion, so that it is needless to dwell here on the points of difference that in all such cases accompany and outweigh the points of likeness. Old Testament prophecy remains, before as after investigation, a thing unique in the world's history.

4. Mohammed's revelations came in his swoons without loss of inner consciousness, his mind being filled with ideas of the unity of God, the resurrection and the judgment. In his swoons sentences seem to be written on his heart and these he recites afterwards. All his revelations are nominally extracts from a heavenly book, presupposing the theory of book revelation, which begins with Ezekiel, but is not elaborated till the Rabbis. Isaiah's lips were purged of sin (Isa. 6.5-7), a word was put in Jeremiah's mouth (Jer. 1.9-10), but Ezekiel *eats* the roll (Ezek. 3.1-3). From this the next step is to Apocalyptic.

SEMITIC POLYTHEISM (1)

Do you remember the time when as children you first read the Old
Testament History? And do you remember being puzzled by what I well
remember was the great puzzle of that history to me? Why were the
Israelites so ready to go aside and worship other gods? What was there
to attract them in the gods of their neighbours? I remind you of this
difficulty now, not that I may answer the question, at least not at
present; but because the very existence of such a difficulty is instructive
as showing how entirely remote our modern habits of thought are from
those in which the polytheism of the ancient Semites had its root. We all
have our doubts and our temptations in matters of faith, but we cannot
imagine ourselves tempted to believe in the Baalim and the Ashtaroth
whose worship had so fatal an attraction for the ancient people of
Jehovah. This entire want of sympathy with the standpoint of Semitic
heathenism is a grave obstacle to the scientific study of the subject. What
we know of the Semitic gods and of the beliefs of their worshippers
concerning them is all fragmentary, and to piece these fragments
together and build up from them a consistent account of Semitic polytheism as a whole it is above all things necessary that we should be able
to put ourselves alongside of the way of thinking to which these strange
deities were conceivable, credible and worthy of worship. If we carry
our own modern habits of religious thought into the study we shall be
liable at every moment to put a false construction on the facts before us
and draw inferences that the old heathen worshippers did not and could
not draw.

A great deal of what has been written about Semitic heathenism is
vitiated by the neglect of this caution and especially by the importation
of modern metaphysical ideas where such ideas have no place. But to
keep our enquiry free from illegitimate presuppositions it is not enough
to be chary in the use of modern ideas and categories. Much of our

knowledge about the gods of the Semites comes to us from Classical writers who saw the facts through a halo of Greek metaphysic, or at all events were apt to read them in the light of their own religious beliefs. Even the oldest Greek writers are fond of identifying foreign with Hellenic deities, as when Herodotus (1.131) tells us that the heavenly Aphrodite is called Mylitta by the Assyrians, Alilat by the Arabs, and Mitra by the Persians. The Phoenicians who sojourned in Greece readily fell in with this habit, as many bilingual inscriptions testify; and when the Greeks became masters of Western Asia, the identification of Hellenic and Semitic deities was carried out on a great scale and was accompanied in many cases by an actual fusion of Asiatic and European cults.

The consequences of all this for the modern study of the Semitic religions has been that too many Greek ideas have been introduced into what has been written on the subject. I do not mean that enquirers have been blind to the difference between Greek gods and the Semitic deities with which they are identified by ancient writers, but rather that the categories of Hellenic thought have dominated the study of Semitic problems in too great a measure. That this should be so was indeed quite natural apart from the colouring already given to Semitic tradition by its transmission through Hellenic authorities: for all European literary culture is profoundly influenced by Greek civilization and the polytheism of Greece is the only heathen system with which modern scholars have, as a rule, had any intimate acquaintance. The gods of Homer and of Phidias are depicted for us in an undying literature, and the visible likeness in which they were conceived by their worshippers is preserved to us in the noblest creations of the plastic art. Thus they make for all of us our ideal of a polytheistic pantheon and the conception of the pre-Christian religion which we derive from these immortal works is naturally present with us when we proceed to the study of less familiar systems. I imagine therefore that it will not be amiss and may serve to clear away misconceptions if I begin what I have to say about the gods of the Semites by indicating some of the main points of contrast between them and the Hellenic deities.

For this purpose it will be sufficient to take the Greek religion as it is known to us by the great works of Classical literature. I do not go back to the beginnings of Greek religion when, so far as we can judge, the distinction between Asiatic and Hellenic belief was much less strongly marked; nor do I take account of the probability that the religion of the uneducated classes in Greece always lagged behind the religion of letters and art. This is a consideration by no means unimportant as accounting for the ready fusion of Eastern and Western cults in the period of the Macedonian empire but it does not affect the matter immediately in hand. For us the religion of Greece is the religion of the cultured classes whose Bible was Homer and whose plastic conception of the gods was that of the Greek sculptors, and it is the difference between this religion and Semitic conceptions of the deities which it is important for us to bear in mind.

The great gods of Greece are sharply discriminated from one another in character, attributes and functions. They form an orderly community under the headship of Zeus, and each member of this community has a recognized sphere of divine activity corresponding to his special tasks and powers. It is true that the parcelling out of the government of the world among the different gods and goddesses is not carried out with strict logical precision upon a single principle, and that conflicts of authority sometimes occur in Olympus, but on the whole Zeus maintains tolerable order in his divine family.

The main cause of discord among the gods is their interest in par-ticular families and communities of men which leads them to take a share in the feuds of humanity. And this again means mainly that Greek religion never entirely shook off the conception that the gods have a natural connection with certain races or certain localities, as Homer's Apollo is the mighty king of Tenedos or as Athena is the special patroness of Athens. But Greek polytheism attained a substantial measure of system and unity by subordinating the local relations of the gods to the conception of special divine functions, which each deity exercised not on behalf of one family or one city, but on behalf of all his worshippers without regard to their descent or birthplace. In a storm at sea the Greek did not invoke his local patron, but Poseidon the god of the Ocean; in sickness he turned to Asklepios, for success in agriculture he called on Demeter, and so forth. Accordingly, we habitually think of the Greek deities not as the gods of particular tribes and towns but as the patrons of certain arts and industries—the powers presiding over certain departments of nature and of human life—and we recognize the character and attributes appropriate to these functions in the portraits of the gods exhibited to us in Greek literature and plastic art.

The theory that each god has his own department gives an air of reasonableness to polytheistic worship. The Greek did not confine his service to a simple patron but addressed himself by turns to all the gods because each could do for his worshipper something that lay outside the province of the other deities. And thus Greek polytheism was not merely a belief in the existence of many gods, but involved the actual worship of many gods in each city and by every citizen. Again, the departmental theory gave to Greek religion a certain character of universality. All the divine powers that preside over nature and human life were represented in the Hellenic pantheon, and within his own sphere each god had a world-wide sway. Even when he went into barbarous lands, the Greek did not feel that he had left Zeus, Apollo and Athena behind him. The sense that the gods of Greece had cosmical and not merely local significance is well brought out in the habitual assumption of Greek travellers that deities of foreign cults are only the Greek deities under other names.

From what has just been said we may fix on three points as characteristic of Greek polytheism in its highest development: (1) Although the gods had certain local connections and special predilections for particular places and people, their power was not limited to one place or their sovereignty to one community of men. (2) Every Greek had access to all the gods, and though in virtue of his descent or his place of residence he might look on one deity as his special patron, it was proper for him to recognize each god in turn according to the nature of his varying needs. (3) The main reason for this was that each god had a special function connected with some particular department of nature or human life. This third point, it will be noted, is the key to the other two, and the whole symmetry and superficial plausibility of the system turns upon it, while on the other hand the essential weakness of the system is that the specialization of divine functions was in point of fact very imperfectly carried out and the offices of the gods overlapped each other at many points to an extent which, apart from all other arguments, might suffice to prove that the origin of Greek polytheism did not lie in the personification of the divine powers working in special departments of nature.

This, however, is by the way. Let us now compare the state of the case as regards the gods of the Semites. There is clear evidence, as was shown in the first course of these lectures, that the oldest Semitic gods were tribal or local. As a rule they were both tribal and local, for the local Baal who had his home in a particular holy place was also the ancestral god of the community that lived around his sanctuary. In this there is probably no fundamental antithesis to the Greek view, for most of the Greek gods had special predilections for particular sanctuaries, and it is highly probable that many of them, though they afterwards assumed a larger character, were originally nothing more than local or tribal deities. But in the case of the Greek gods this is more or less a matter of speculation and probably a majority of enquirers still hold that the greater gods of Hellas were worshipped as cosmical powers by the undivided Aryans long before they found local seats in Hellas. No such position can be maintained with any degree of plausibility as regards the Semitic gods, for here it is very clear that the local connection of the god involves a local limit to his power. The gods of Israel, say the Syrians in 1 Kgs 20.23, are gods of the hills; if we fight against them in the plains we shall be stronger than they. So, again, the Syrian and Babylonian colonists whom Sargon settled in the country of Samaria ascribed the increase of wild beasts in the land to the anger of the god of the country, and asked for a Hebrew priest to teach them how to worship Jehovah. They had indeed brought their own idols with them, but these were no match for the god of the land upon his own ground (2 Kgs 17.24-28). Similarly in Arabia, in the times of heathenism, we are told that a traveller halting for the night in some desert valley would say, 'I take refuge with the Mighty One of this valley from the demons of the night and everything harmful that is near.'[1] The unknown local power, not the man's own ancestral god, is the proper helper against local malign influences.

In Semitic heathenism and especially in the Baal worship of the Northern Semites we can see that the connection of the gods with particular places was of a physical kind. The energy of the god had its centre at the sanctuary where a holy fountain or stream or grave was revered as instinct with divine life; it was here that the worshippers appeared before their god with gestures of adoration and gifts of homage, and all the blessings which he conferred appeared in some sort to emanate from this centre. At a distance from the sanctuary the god was less powerful, as his habitual energy did not extend beyond his own land (i.e. the land of his worshippers, the community of his sanctuary). A man who left his own people and settled abroad left his god behind him and was compelled to become the client of a new worship.

What I have described is the primitive type of local Baal-worship as it is found among the agricultural populations of Canaan and Syria, in the oldest times of which we have record. It is a type that could not be

---

1. Ibn Hishām's edition of Ibn Isḥāq, *Life of Mohammed*, pp. 130-31.

maintained unmodified except in a society of very simple structure where the country was divided up among small communities, living in comparative isolation and vegetating, so to speak, from generation to generation, each on its ancestral soil. The physical conditions of Syria, where small regions of great fertility are separated by barren tracts and rough mountains, favoured the existence of such communities, many of which remained almost untouched by outside influence long after the few great routes that intersected the country were full of international traffic and familiar with the tread of Assyrian and Persian hosts. It is in these remote and isolated spots that we must look for the oldest type of Syrian religion, and sound method demands that we should examine this type fully and learn all we can from it before we attempt to deal with the more complex religious phenomena exhibited in the cults of great empires like Assyria or great merchant cities like those of Phoenicia, which lay on the highways of international movement.

Let us then enquire whether we can realize to ourselves more precisely how the power and activity of the god was conceived as radiating outwards from his sanctuary. In some cases the conception appears to have been almost purely physical. A community of one worship occupies the basin of a single stream—such as the Adonis in Lebanon; the chief seat of the god is at the sacred source and the sphere of his lifegiving activity extends as far as the blessed waters flow. But the anthropomorphic conception of the god as king gave room for wider conceptions. Wherever the people went to extend their borders by occupying waste lands or encroaching on the territories of their neighbours the god went with them, and the mere fact that they were able to establish themselves on new ground was sufficient evidence that they were still within the region over which their god had effective sway. If in this way a considerable stretch of country came to be included in the dominion of one god, his sanctuaries might be multiplied; for it is not in the nature of Semitic heathenism that a man should realize his dependence on a god to whom he had not constant and easy access at a holy place. Thus among the Moabites the national god Chemosh had a sanctuary at Kerioth (Curayyāt), Mesha built another for him at Dibon, and doubtless he was worshipped also at other high places throughout the land, as Jehovah was worshipped in the local high places of Israel.

I think we can see that when the same god came to be worshipped simultaneously at many sanctuaries and was held to be present at them all, a distinct step was taken towards a larger conception of the divine nature than that which is involved in the worship of the Baal of a single sanctuary. And from our point of view we may be apt to think that a god who can be present in many places at once is on the fair way to become omnipresent and shake off all local limitation. But it must be remembered that in the ordinary service of a local sanctuary there was little or nothing to impress upon the worshippers the idea that the god whom they adored at their local altar was the god of the whole land. In a general way, no doubt, they believed that he was so, as the peasants of an Italian village believe that their Madonna is the Madonna of the Catholic world. But the main point was that he was their local god dwelling in their midst who might be reckoned on to take their part, not only against the enemies of the nation, but likewise in purely local matters, as in feuds with the people of a neighbouring town. In ordinary times this point of view would vastly outweigh the larger conception of Jehovah or Chemosh as the national god: for it is very evident from what we know of Semitic history that communal feeling was ordinarily far stronger than national feeling. Further, it must be remembered that the forms of worship at all sanctuaries were of a type that directly suggested a physical connection between the god and the holy place where he dwelt in a sacred fountain or tree or pillar. This was a palpable notion easily grasped by everyone, while the notion that the same god had his seat at distant holy places was hard to grasp and lay outside the region of daily experience. And finally, it must be remembered that the local sanctuaries of which Israel or Moab became possessed by conquest, had for the most part been the holy places of Canaanite communities before the conquest, and that the new worship was deeply coloured by the old. For the Israelites we know this as a matter of history, and the prophets depict the worship of Jehovah at the high places as to all intents and purposes the worship of a multitude of Canaanite Baalim. In other states formed by conquest the conditions cannot have been different, for in the nature of things the centres of agricultural population would remain the same before and after the conquest.

On the whole, therefore, the multiplication of sanctuaries of a single god cannot, in the older period of Semitic history, have done much to break down the notion of the physical connection of the god with a local centre. The tendency was rather to break up the national deity into a multitude of special forms, each of which was practically the Baal of a single commune or city. To a certain extent this tendency was counteracted by the association of religion with all the public functions of national life, in which men from many communes appeared at the sanctuary together. But as government was very little centralized, except for purposes of national defence, it was mainly in time of war that there was occasion for acts of national worship—the Jehovah of the Hebrews, you will remember, has for his favourite title *yahweh ṣᵉbā'ôt*—Jehovah the god of the armies of Israel. When the independent states of Western Asia fell before the Assyrians, this way of keeping national feeling alive came to an end and civic or communal worship gained a still greater predominance. But to some extent the sense of religious oneness between larger circles of worshippers was still kept alive, in another way, by the operation of the very same habit of thought which we have hitherto contemplated as a disintegrating force. The idea that each god has a physical connection with one sanctuary and its district naturally produces the conception that, however widely his influence may extend, and however his sanctuaries may be multiplied, the true centre of his divine energy and the place where he is nearest to the prayers of his worshippers is still his old, primaeval seat; the new sanctuaries are not as good as the old from which, to quote the language of an inscription at Baetocaece to which I shall have to return later, 'the power of the god proceeds'.[2]

Hence men who were in great need, or who sought to commend themselves to their god in a special way, were not content with the regular worship of their own local sanctuary but made pilgrimages also to the ancient shrine of their ancestral deity. The practice of pilgrimage is mostly known to us from the records of a comparatively late date, when the old nationalities and their national faiths had broken down and when men were no longer content with their own gods but were eager to seek more powerful helpers outside. But there can, I think, be no reasonable doubt that the beginnings of the practice are very ancient and are to be sought within the domain of national religion. Thus in the land of Israel we can see that the holy places that received most honour were those which claimed to date from patriarchal times,[3] and in the time of Amos pilgrimages were made from Mt Ephraim to the distant sanctuary of Beersheba (Amos 5.5). Of the sentiment that prompted the pilgrims we have a remarkable illustration in the journey of Elijah to Sinai, that there he might meet Jehovah face to face in his primaeval sanctuary. For in

2.   Le Bas and Waddington, *Voyage archéologique en Grèce et en Asie Mineure*, p. 2720a.

3.   Dan is an exception, but it was at least a very old high place with great traditions.

the ancient poetry of Israel, in the song of Deborah and the Blessing of Moses (Judg. 5.4; Deut. 33.2), Sinai is the centre of Jehovah's working, where he gathers his storm-clouds and the lightnings, his fiery ministers, when he sets forth to display himself in glory to his people Israel. The same feeling, that to keep in full touch with the God one must also keep in touch with his oldest sanctuary, appears in the patriarchal history. It is the same narrator (E) who in Gen. 33.20 tells us that Jacob built an altar at Shechem and in ch. 35 calls him to Bethel to do worship at the shrine where God had just revealed himself to him in his flight to Syria. And this feeling is common to all the Semites. In Arabia, as Wellhausen has observed,[4] a tribe that entirely abandoned its old seats seems generally to have left its old god behind and taken up the local worship of the region in which it is settled. In Samaria, in like manner, the foreign colonists introduced by Sargon, though at first they brought their own idols with them, became in the long run exclusive worshippers of Jehovah. Once more the idol of Nana of Erech was carried off at a very early date by the king of Elam and remained in honour in his kingdom for many centuries. Yet the kings of Elam continued to send gifts of homage to Erech, her ancient seat.[5] But perhaps the most instructive example is that of Tyrian colonies. Whenever the seamen of Tyre planted their factories they carried with them the worship of the Tyrian Melqart and set up temples and altars in his honour. But it was still deemed a sacred duty to send gifts of homage to the temple of the mother-city. When the Carthaginians were hard pressed by Agathocles, they judged that the chief cause of their misfortune was the wrath of Heracles—not because they had been remiss to do him service in his Carthaginian temple but because they had been niggardly with the sacred tribute due to his temple at Tyre.[6] Amidst all his wanderings their god was still above all things the god of Tyre and claimed to be acknowledged as such by acts of homage paid to his ancient seat. The political supremacy of Tyre was short-lived, but her religious supremacy as the centre of Melqart's sovereignty lasted as long as the worship of the god. In the remotest parts of the Roman world we meet with inscriptions that celebrate the Heracles of Tyre under his local title,[7] or

---

4. Wellhausen, *Reste arabischen Heidentumes*, p. 182.

5. C.P. Tiele, *Babylonisch-assyrische Geschichte* II (Gotha: F.A. Perthes, 1888), p. 378.

6. Diodorus Siculus, 20.14.

7. Even in Britain (G. Kaibel [ed.] *Inscriptiones Italiae et Siciliae* [Inscriptiones

record the continued religious intercourse between the Tyrians abroad and the ancient seat of their faith.[8]

'Tyre', says Renan,[9] in a passage that is perhaps somewhat over-charged but contains a substantial element of truth, 'Tyre, like Jerusalem, was the centre of a religion whose adepts, organized in confraternities of Heraclists, and diffused all over the Mediterranean, had their eyes unceasingly turned to their central and unique temple, made pilgrimages there, and thither sent their gifts of homage.' The parallel here drawn between Jerusalem and Tyre, between the Jews of the diaspora and the Heraclists of the Roman empire, may easily be pressed too far. The grand distinction between Judaism and the other faiths of the Roman empire lay in the fact that the Jews knew no holy place except Jerusalem. The Tyrians set up altars to Melqart wherever they went, the Jews of the dispersion had no regular worship save that of the synagogue and kept their faith alive without image, altar or sacrifice. For the history of religion this distinction is vastly more important than the parallel on which Renan insists between the significance attached by each people to its ancestral and central temple. But the parallel itself is just and touches the point in which the religion of Israel failed to detach itself completely from the physical substratum that underlies all Semitic heathenism. This point is of so much interest that we may pause for a moment to examine it in the light of the Old Testament history. You are aware that it was the ritual of the synagogue, not of the temple, that prepared the way for Christian worship, with its entire negation of the idea that God is nearer at one place than at another if only he be worshipped in spirit and in truth. Again the institution of the synagogue (insofar as it is a place of prayer and not merely a school of the sacred law) was the fruit of the doctrine that for Israel there is but one lawful place of sacrifice. The reformers to whom we owe the Pentateuch and who made it their object to give practical expression to the spiritual ideas of the prophets, took as their starting point the abolition of the local high places and the

Graecae XIV, Berlin: G. Reimarus, 1890], 2554 = *CIG* 6806). A notable inscription of earlier date is the bilingual *CIS* 1.122 from 'the port of Heracles' in Malta where the god is described as 'our lord Melqart, Baal of Tyre'—in the Greek *Heraklēs archēgetēs*. The Sidonians in Greece in like manner kept up the worship of the Baal of Sidon; see the Piraeus inscription of 96 BC.

8. See especially the inscription from Puteoli (Kaibel, *Inscriptiones Italiae et Siciliae*, 830 = *CIG* 5853).

9. E. Renan, *Mission de Phénicie* (Paris: Imprimerie Impériale, 1864), pp. 574-75. [ET by W.R.S.]

concentration of all ritual at Jerusalem. It has often been pointed out that this plan, as it was first set forth in the book of Deuteronomy and further built upon in the later Priestly legislation, is not in exact accordance with the ideas of the greatest prophets, to whom all ritual is substantially indifferent and Jerusalem is the centre of Jehovah's activity only because it is the centre of the nation in and through which he works out his transcendent purpose in human history. The central sanctuary of the Pentateuch with its daily and annual cycle of sacrifices, in which the mass of the people have no direct part, but only watch it from afar with their mind's eye while their own daily religion is wholly without ritual—this central sanctuary, I say, remained to Judaism not as a legitimate development of Isaiah's teaching but essentially as a compromise between the old and the new, the old Semitic tradition of worship and the new doctrine of the spiritual service of righteousness in which all ritual acts are indifferent.

In the book of Deuteronomy and the cognate parts of the Old Testament, the connection between the temple worship and the old tradition that the activity of the national god must have a local centre and starting point is reduced to a minimum and all merely physical conceptions are as far as possible excluded by the emphasis with which it is proclaimed that Jehovah has no natural connection with Jerusalem, with the land of Canaan, or even with the nation of Israel. All is of his own free choice, the sanctuary is but the place which he has chosen to set his name there and which he is as free to leave again as he was to choose it. But it is certain from Jeremiah 7 that the mass of those who accepted Josiah's reformation were not prepared for this teaching and trusted to the temple of Jerusalem as a pledge of Jehovah's continued presence and favour exactly as the Tyrians trusted in their ancient temple of Melqart.

In comparison with Beersheba or Shechem or Hebron, Jerusalem was but a modern holy place, but its dignity as the capital, its long connection with the Ark and the Davidic dynasty, its comparative immunity from the ravages of war at a time when almost every other sanctuary of Jehovah had once and again been plundered or laid in ruins, had gradually transferred to it in the popular imagination the prerogative of being the especial seat of Jehovah, as Sinai had been of old (cf. Ps. 68.18, ET 17). Even in the time of Amos it is from Jerusalem that the voice of Jehovah proceeds which withers the forests of Carmel (Amos 1.2), and in Ps. 20.3 (ET 2), which it is hardly possible to refer to a post-exilic date, it is from the temple of Zion that Jehovah sends forth the help that gives victory to his king. In these expressions we may recognize a figurative element, but the figure is of the type which consists in retaining in the language of poetry phrases that were originally used in a literal sense and have not yet ceased to appeal to the popular imagination. To the mass of the Hebrews in the time of Jeremiah all such phrases were more than mere metaphor and implied that Jehovah was really nearer at Zion than elsewhere. This is precisely the kind of belief on which the pratice of pilgrimage to heathen shrines was based, and it was the existence of this belief, and with it doubtless of a well-established practice of pilgrimage to Jerusalem, before the time of Josiah's reformation, that made it possible for that king to carry through the abolition of the high places. It is plain that the pilgrims from Shechem, Shiloh and Samaria, of whom we read in Jer. 41.5, were not drawn to Jerusalem by obedience to Judaean law but by the same impulse which from the days of the Assyrian conquest and downwards led all the Semites to seek in pilgrimage to famous shrines a necessary supplement to the rites of local worship that no longer sufficed to provide for their religious cravings. And so, though on one side the religion of Israel was finally cut off from the old materialistic basis of heathenism by the abolition of the local high places, it still kept in touch with the lower Semitic faiths in retaining the temple of Jerusalem as the visible centre of Jehovah's sovereignty. Even the early Christian church did not break the last bond that tied it to the system of antique religion till the flames that consumed the temple of Zion flashed forth the signal that Jehovah had no longer a distinctive dwelling place on earth.

I have dwelt so long on the local relations of the gods that I fear I have already tried your patience; but there are still one or two points that must be touched upon before we pass from the subject. Among the Greeks two conceptions seem to have operated to loosen the connection between the gods and particular local sanctuaries. The older of these is the conception which we find in Homer that the gods, in addition to their local haunts, have a common dwelling place in Olympus from which they overlook the world. And in later times considerable influence must be assigned to the identification of the chief deities with astral powers, the sun, the moon, the planets and so forth. How do the Semitic religions stand in these respects? It is generally supposed that a Semitic Olympus is alluded to in Isa. 14.13, where the king of Babylon is introduced as saying in his heart, 'I will ascend into heaven, above the stars of El will I set my throne, I will sit in the Mountain of tryst, in the uttermost North.' This passage dates from the Babylonian Captivity and evidently refers to a Babylonian belief, though Assyriologists are not yet agreed as to the nature of the belief referred to, some identifying the Mountain of tryst with the mountain Arallu, while one of the latest and ablest writers on the subject[10] entirely rejects this view. But as the Babylonians and Assyrians had a much more developed Pantheon than the other Semites, we can in no case be justified in speaking of a Semitic Olympus, even if it should ultimately prove that there was a Babylonian mountain of the gods where all the deities met together. Still less is it legitimate to build on the analogous conceptions that are found among the Indians, the Persians and other races that lay far beyond the Semitic horizon. The passage in Isaiah proves nothing for Hebrew belief and I cannot understand how so cautious a scholar as Dillmann allows himself in his commentary thereon to speak of 'the conception of the seat of the gods, which in Israel had almost disappeared under the influence of Jahvism'.[11] What is certain is that, if there ever was such a conception, it never took such shape as to modify in the smallest degree the conception of the local seats of the gods.[12]

And now as to heavenly gods. The worship of sun, moon and planets plays a very great part in Babylonian religion and many of the great gods are either directly identified with heavenly bodies or closely associated with them. This Babylonian belief and the astrological theories that went with it had a great influence on all the later forms of Semitic religion and especially on all theosophy; but how far the western Semites identified their gods with astral powers *before* the Assyrian period it is hard to say. Such general statements as that of Jensen,[13] 'Alle Nordsemiten haben ursprünglich als höchsten Gott den Himmelsherrn und Sonnenherrn', are totally unsupported by evidence. That the older Canaanite Baalim are telluric rather than heavenly powers appears very clearly from the use of the term 'Baal's land', which denotes, not as used to be thought, land watered by the rains of heaven, but land made independent of irrigation by a moist bottom. And this view goes far more naturally with the doctrine of the local connections of the godhead

10. Jensen, *Die Kosmologie der Babylonier*, p. 454.

11. A. Dillmann, *Der Prophet Jesaia* (Leipzig: S. Hirzel, 1890), p. 137. [ET by W.R.S.]

12. Neither Ps. 48.3 (ET 2) nor Ezek. 28.14 adds anything to the argument.

13. Jensen, *Kosmologie*, p. 454.

than the theory that the Baal was always the sun god, the lord of heaven. But the practical point to be considered here is that, even in the period when the more famous gods were generally conceived as heavenly powers, the conception that their power on earth radiated from a local centre persisted unimpaired. The classical proof of this is the inscription of Baetocaece already cited,[14] in which the god whose power proceeds from that village is yet designated as the 'heavenly Zeus'. Those who are able to do so may believe, if they please, that the Baal of Baetocaece was adored as a heavenly god before his working on earth was tied to a local centre, but it is not open to anyone, after this evidence, to imagine that because a Semitic god has heavenly predicates he ceases to be in the strictest sense tied to a local centre of activity.

Another topic of great interest connected with the local limitations of deity is the use of portable idols, and in general the question of the material means and processes used in connection with the movements of the gods from place to place. We have seen that it was not an easy thing to detach a god entirely from his ancient seat; but he could be induced to accompany his people when they went forth to battle or even to join a party of colonists and take up a new, though for the most part only a secondary, residence in their new home. In all such cases there is a kind of conflict between the two conceptions of the god of a place, and the god of a race of men. The Semitic gods were both, and when the men moved away from the old sanctuary, the two conceptions no longer covered one another. On the whole, as would appear from the foregoing discussion, locality proved stronger than race, and those who were wholly cut off from the old sanctuary found themselves constrained to take to themselves new gods. But there was always an effort to avoid this and it is in such dilemmas that the ingenuity of a primitive people loves to display itself in the invention of some contrivance to bridge over a logical difficulty.

Among the older Semites the special mark of the presence of the god in his sanctuary was the *maṣṣēbâ* or sacred stone, which served at once as altar and idol, and the Asherah, the sacred tree or pole. These were symbols of the godhead, not in any metaphysical sense, but because it was believed that the sacrificial blood and other offerings brought into contact with them were actually conveyed to the god and brought into contact with him. The god was present in the stone or tree when he was duly called upon. But he was not always there; for he might be moving

14. See n. 2 above.

about engaged in various business or he might be absent at another sanctuary if he had more altars than one. Thus the priests of Baal on Mt Carmel find it necessary to summon the god by loud invocations and other more potent means (1 Kgs 18.26-29). And at some sanctuaries there were seasons when the deity was supposed to be away from home. At the great Astarte temple of Eryx the sacred doves used to leave the temple every year and were supposed to accompany the goddess to Libya. After nine days they returned headed by a dove of purple or golden colour which was probably identified with Astarte herself. The departure was celebrated in the feast of the *Anagōgia*, 'Embarkation', and the return in that of the *Katagōgia*, 'Debarkation', which was observed with universal rejoicing and clapping of hands (*krotalizousin meta charas*, says Athenaeus,[15] and cf. Ps. 47.2 [ET 1] and the hand-clapping at the accession of Jehoash in 2 Kgs 11.12).

When a private person was called away to a distance from the sanctuary by business or by war, his proper course was to commend himself to the care of his god by a vow to be discharged on his return. This is the old Hebrew custom, as we see in the case of Jacob at Bethel (Gen. 28.20-22), and the same practice prevailed in Arabia. While the man was absent he let his hair grow long and on his return to his own city he cut it off at the sanctuary. In the interval he could enjoy no formal access to the deity and had no material pledge of the presence and help of his god save such as might be got by carrying on his person some sacred relic, amulet or tiny image in which a portion of the divine virtue was thought to reside. The use of such charms was very widely spread in all antiquity and turns up in unexpected quarters. Even in the armies of the Maccabees there were Jews who carried under their shirts small consecrated objects, probably images of the idols of the Philistine city of Jamnia (2 Macc. 12.40). But the use of charms has its origin in a lower form of religion than that with which we are now concerned, and even where the amulet took the form of an image, it was hardly regarded as a symbol of the actual presence of the god but simply as being physically charged with a certain amount of sacred supernatural potency. I am inclined to think that the same thing is true of the larger images which the Bedouins used to buy in Mecca and set up at their doors, touching them with their hands as they went out and in, and also of the teraphim

15. Athenaeus, *The Deipnosophists*, 9. 394-5, e.g., followed by Claudius Aelianus, *Varia Historia*, 1.15. For the dove of the colour of 'purple' or 'golden' Aphrodite, cf. Claudius Aelianus, *De natura animalium*, 4.2.

used in Canaan. These household images were rather amulets on a larger scale than gods in the full sense of the word.[16] It does not seem that they were honoured by formal sacrifices or identified with the national god of their owners. In old Israel we find teraphim not only in private hands, but at the sanctuaries of Jehovah, where they were used in connection with the 'ephod' as a means of divination. But here they are part of the subordinate furniture of the holy place; teraphim alone without an ephod or a graven image or both are not enough to constitute a holy place.[17] One may indeed suspect that the private teraphim of the Israelites were in many cases relics of the old gentile worships quite distinct from the religion of Jehovah.

In great public expeditions of a protracted kind something more than this was needed; the national god must go forth with his people and be accessible during the campaign in acts of public worship or when an oracle was required for the conduct of the business in hand. This requisite was met by the institution of portable sanctuaries of which the Ark and its Tabernacle are the most familiar example. Similarly, as we learn from Diodorus Siculus, 20.25, the Carthaginian army was accompanied by a sacred tent beside which an altar was erected on which the most comely of the prisoners was sacrificed after a victory. Presumably the tent contained the images of the gods, who, in the language of a document preserved by Polybius,[18] 'made the campaign along with' the army. The sacrifices of the Babylonians on their campaigns are referred to in Ezekiel 21, and an Assyrian monument from Khorsabād depicts the portable altar, the sacred pole and other furniture that were used on such occasions.

The invention of portable sanctuaries and especially of portable idols may possibly go back to the nomadic Semites and to a time when the gods were still tribal rather than local. But the probabilities are all against such a view. There is less trace of such an institution in Arabia than in any other part of the Semitic world, and nowhere else is the principle so

16. Laban, however, calls them 'his gods': Gen 31.30.

17. I fancy that the domestic teraphim without an ephod were not sufficient even for divination, for till Abiathar joined him with the ephod David was guided by the soothsayer, while from that time forth he used the priestly oracle. Teraphim without ephod are mentioned as a means of divination only in late passages (2 Kgs 23.24; Zech. 10.2). In Ezek. 21.26 the name seems to be applied to the portable idols that accompanied the Babylonians on their campaigns. [W.R.S. wrongly wrote 'Assyrians' for 'Babylonians' here.—J.D.]

18. Polybius, 7.9.

strongly marked that a tribe that changes its seats changes its gods. Even the Ark of Jehovah is not carried back by Hebrew tradition to patriarchal times; the patriarchs do worship only where they have a fixed altar.[19] It is therefore more likely that portable symbols of the godhead first arose among the settled Semites and in connection with the religion of the army in war. In this connection the idea of a portable god involves no great breach with the conception that each deity has a local home, for when the campaign is over the god returns to his temple. But when the notion of portable gods was once established, its application could easily be extended and would serve to smooth away the difficulty of establishing new permanent sanctuaries in conquered regions or colonies over the sea. A Greek colony always carried its gods with it and it is probable that this was often done by the Phoenician colonists also.[20] Even in Israel we find that the sanctuary of Jehovah at Dan was constituted by setting up the image from Micah's sanctuary (Judg. 18.30), just as David gave a religious character to his new capital by transferring the Ark to it.

19. There is no real parallel between the Arabic '*otfa* (A. Blunt, *Bedouin Tribes of the Euphrates* II [London: John Murray, 1879], p. 146, cf. C.M. Doughty, *Travels in Arabia Deserta* [Cambridge: Cambridge University Press, 1888] I, p. 61 and II, p. 304) and the Ark of the covenant. Compare rather Ayisha's litter at the battle of the Camel (AD 656).

20. It is, however, noteworthy that at Paphos the idol is a *cippus*. Was it carried from Phoenicia as Naaman asks for Hebrew earth to worship Jehovah on? Naaman's earth seems the more primitive way of moving a Baal-sanctuary. Try to find parallels.

Third Series, Lecture 2

SEMITIC POLYTHEISM (2)

The Greek had access to all Hellenic gods, and in practice worshipped all as fit occasion arose. If he acknowledged one god as his special patron, he did this in no exclusive sense. All the gods of Greece were his gods. Among the Semites this unity of religion was never attained. There was no pan-Semitic feeling like the pan-Hellenic feeling that united the Greeks of different states in a common religious life, in spite of their political feuds. When two Semitic states were at war their gods were at war also, and when one state crushed another it ravaged its sanctuaries and destroyed its idols or carried them off in captivity, not to be worshipped but to stand as trophies in the temples of their captors.[1] This was the standing practice of the Assyrians, and in like manner the Philistines carry off the Ark to set it up in the temple of Dagon, and Mesha dedicates to Chemosh the spoils of the Israelite places. So when David burns the idols of the Philistines (2 Sam. 5.21) or robs the Ammonite Malkam of his crown (2 Sam. 12.30) he is only following the ordinary rule of Semitic warfare.

The heathen Semites did not deny that the gods of other nations were real gods and powerful on their proper ground; but they had no occasion to worship them, for their native gods were sufficient masters in their own country and they had no reason to think that their homage would reach the ear of gods that dwelt far off, or that if it did reach them it would find acceptance with the hereditary deities of foreigners and enemies. You see how broad is the distinction between this point of view and that of the Greeks with whom the conviction that the same gods ruled in all lands was so strong that they detected Greek deities

---

1. W. Lotz (ed.), *Die Inschriften Tiglathpileser's, I* (Leipzig: J.C. Hinrichs, 1880), p. 37 para. 19 is a good example = Schrader (ed.), *Keilinschriftliche Bibliothek* I (1889), p. 29. See also Asshurbanipal's annals, *passim*. Contrast the conduct of Alexander, who sacrifices to Melqart on capturing Tyre.

under foreign names whenever they visited a strange country. When Alexander took Tyre by storm he did sacrifice to Melqart; a Semitic conqueror would have burned the temple.

The Semitic principle that no man has anything to do with the gods that are outside of his own political and social community subsisted, practically unimpaired, till the rise of the great empires put an end to the independence of the smaller states, and made men feel that their local gods were too weak to be effective helpers. And as the independent communities were for the most part very small there was no room in them for the development of a rich, polytheistic cultus. In antiquity worship implies a sanctuary, a ritual, a system of sacrificial feasts, and these are costly things which cannot be multiplied in a small community consisting, as was mostly the case, of a simple town with its fields and villages. As a rule such a community had one temple and one altar, a simple worship of a local god or goddess (or more commonly of a divine pair, the local Baal and his partner) to whom all sacrifices and vows were addressed and by whose name all oaths were taken, and at whose mouth oracles were sought. In addition to this official worship there were no doubt many minor practices of superstition at sacred wells and trees or the like. And the richer families might often have teraphim or household idols to which some form of domestic homage was paid. But these minor superstitions hardly come into account here: they formed no part of the public religion and can hardly have been associated with the name of any other god than the local Baal. Broadly speaking the local Baal had to do for his people everything that a god can do for men: there was no room for a differentiation of functions such as we find in Greece. Nor was there much room for ascribing to him any well-marked individuality of character. For every little Canaanite community lived and thought like its neighbours. They all had the same round of daily life, the same needs and wishes to bring before their god, the same forms of sacrifice and ritual. Their gods, therefore, were all cast in the same general mould, and to us they are indistinguishable from one another except by their local connections. In many cases the various local gods are not known to us even by separate names, but only by titles, as the Baal of this or that place. They may often have had distinctive names in addition to those titles (many Semitic god-names are known to us only from theophoric proper names), but for the most part these were hardly used except perhaps in naming of children after their god. In ordinary life the local god was simply 'the Lord, the King, the

Lady'. These terms were sufficiently distinctive because the worshipper acknowledged only one Lady and one Lord.

It would appear, then, that as a rule each of the smaller Semitic communities worshipped only one god or one syzygy consisting of a god and a goddess. This result of our enquiry is somewhat startling, for one of the best established results of the comparative study of early societies is that the smallest local communities always consist of a plurality of gentes and that each gens has its gentile worship. I do not doubt that this was so among the Semites also in prehistoric times and that traces of this primitive structure of society survived, both in the religious and in the political order, into the historical period. But I think it is clear on the face of the facts that the later Semitic polytheism is not the direct descendant of gentile worship, that is that when in later times we find in a great city temples of many gods, these are not the gods of the several gentes that were represented among its original inhabitants. As a rule, at least, the old gentile faiths survived only in obscure superstitions such as the worship of teraphim, and the full status of god was reserved for the local Baal, who may originally have been identified with the god of a particular clan (as indeed the existence of hereditary priesthoods makes it probable that he often was), but who was essentially the potent god of the *place* as well as of the people. And this local god became also the hereditary god of all the inhabitants of the place because all the gentes traced themselves up to one common stock, as indeed the various gentes of one local community habitually learn to do after the establishment of the law of kinship through males. For the smaller Semitic communities we may take it as the rule that each community had one god or pair of gods who were at once gods of the place and the hereditary gods of its inhabitants. In the larger Semitic communities the state of religion was not so simple. Such communities were formed in more than one way, and in each case the nature of the political ties that bound the local communes together had an influence on the national religion. But in all cases we may take them as formed out of smaller communities of the type already characterized.

The simplest case of all has already been considered: that namely where a homogeneous nation extends its frontiers by conquest or colonization and carries its religion along with it. In such cases, as we have seen, there was a tendency to break up the national deity into a multitude of local forms. Chemosh, for example, would be worshipped in one place as the Baal of Kerioth, in another as the Baal of Dibon; but all Moabites would have access to both sanctuaries and feel that at both they were worshipping the same god.[2] To produce out of such conditions a holy theism of the Greek type would have required a very extraordinary and indeed an incredible combination of circumstances. I will not waste time in following this out in detail, but will say at once that beyond question the worship of many gods side by side, where it occurs among the Semites, is due to the combination in one state of elements that are not homogeneous.

Many of the larger Semitic nations were mere federations, in which each tribe or city retained its autonomous life, though all acted together for common defence or other specified purposes. Such federations were common in ancient Arabia and they represent the highest measure of political unity to which the nomadic Semites commonly attained. Similar confederations appear to have existed among the Canaanites at the time of the Hebrew invasion, and are found at a later date among the Philistines, with their league of five cities, and among the Phoenicians of the Persian period. The formation of such a union would not call on the communities comprised in it to give up their own sanctuaries and gods; but according to antique ideas the league of the worshippers implied a league between the gods they adored. And from this the step was easy to a certain amount of common worship; for when the people went out together for battle their gods went with them, and when they met for council or to celebrate a victory, a common religious service could not fail to take place. The idols of the Philistines which David burned (2 Sam. 5.21) were doubtless the idols of the various cantons engaged in the war and would enjoy common honours from the whole host. Again, when the lords of the Philistines met to rejoice over the taking of Samson, they offered sacrifice together in the temple of Dagon (Judg. 16.23). And apart from such public occasions it is reasonable to suppose that a Philistine leaving his native city to reside for a time in another town of the league would not be excluded from its religion. And finally, whenever a long alliance between two neighbouring cities made inter-marriages frequent, many persons would have through their parents an interest in the worship of two sanctuaries.

What took place in a federation like that of the Philistines might also take place in trading cities through the operation of merely commercial

2.   There was a break-up of national feeling to an extent that allowed the local gods to become quite distinct and even lose their common name, and yet persistence of the idea that every Moabite had an interest in each sanctuary and its god.

treaties granting rights of hospitality to foreign merchants. Here also we may suppose that certain religious privileges would be conceded to foreign residents, who yet would not break off connection with their old religion, and that mixed marriages would carry the religious union a step further. But the motives to a fusion of religion would naturally be strongest where several cities came to be united not by a federal bond but under a single kingdom, and this is the quarter to which one naturally looks for the beginnings of polytheism in the full sense of the word; that is, for a public religion in which many gods—originally all the local gods of particular cities—are all raised to the ranks of national deities and are worshipped by all members of the state as occasion serves, both in their old local sanctuaries and in new temples, erected in the capital and in other cities under the influence of the comprehensive national faith.

It is generally admitted that the polytheism of the Assyrian empire is a case in point. Here the inscriptions show us that many gods were habitually invoked together in all matters of national importance. Thus Asshurbanipal makes war by the command of Asshur, Bilit, Sin, Shamash, Ramman, Bel, Nebo, Ishtar of Nineveh, the Queen of Kidmuru, Ishtar of Arbela, Ninip, Nergal and Nusku—a goodly pantheon.[3] Of some of these deities it is known with certainty, and of others it is highly probable, that they were originally the local gods of particular cities included in the Assyrian state. They all would have been worshipped by the king because his power rested on the union of all these cities in one homogeneous kingdom. It cannot be supposed that all the gods in this long list received regular service from the mass of the people, for ancient worship, in the full sense of the word, implies a sanctuary and altar, and the common folk would ordinarily confine their worship to the nearest shrine; but all were acknowledged by the king and his court; temples in honour of all the great gods seem to have been erected in the principal towns; and the priestly theology or theosophy took account of them all.

It does not appear from the evidence open to us that anything like the copious Assyrian pantheon existed in early times in other parts of the Semitic world. Nowhere else indeed do we meet with the political conditions to which Babylonia and Assyria owed the multitude of their gods, *viz.* a centralized or durable empire resting on an ancient civilization and comprehending a multitude of great cities whose local worships had taken full shape and acquired individual character before they were

---

3.　See Schrader (ed.), *Keilinschriftliche Bibliothek* II (1890), p. 157.

gathered up into the national religion. This fact alone would be enough to account for a great difference between the development of religion in Assyria and in the smaller states; whether there was a further reason for difference in the ethnic conditions of the region of the two rivers, is not so certain; but most scholars think that the religion of Babylon and Assyria was in great part derived from an earlier non-Semitic race. For my own part I prefer to leave this question open and to direct your attention to the causes which limited the free development of a polytheistic pantheon among the smaller Semitic nations.

We have seen that the first step towards the fusion of local religions was taken wherever two cities or communes were united by a durable covenant for purposes either of war or of commerce. Under such a covenant, especially when its operation was aided by intermarriage, there would be many cases where the member of one community would find admission to the worship of the other without deserting his own faith; he would be the subject of one god and at the same time the client of another. That the idea of religious clientship played a great part in Semitic religion has been proved in the first course of these lectures and appears particularly from the frequency of proper names designating a man as the client of such and such a god. But mere clientship does not go far to establish a full polytheistic system; there is a great difference between worshipping the god of another place when one happens to visit his sanctuary and the habitual worship of two gods. Polytheism in the full sense of the word exists only where a community habitually worships a number of gods, including them all among its national deities and honouring them all with temples, feasts and the other recognized signs of national homage. The clearest evidence of developed polytheism is got where we find in one city not merely the temple of one local god or of a god and goddess but of several gods and goddesses.

Of the way in which temples of various gods might come to be set up side by side we have instructive examples in the Old Testament in the history of Solomon and of Ahab. In each instance the introduction of a new worship with its altars and ritual is the work of the monarch and stands in direct connection with his foreign policy. Thus when we are told that Solomon erected sanctuaries outside Jerusalem to the Sidonian Astarte, the Moabite Chemosh and the Ammonite Melech or Malkam (1 Kgs 11.4-8; 2 Kgs 23.13) in order to please his foreign wives, we must remember that his numerous marriages were themselves dictated by policy and may fairly conclude that he sought to strengthen the relations of Israel with allied and subject states both by matrimonial alliances and by giving aliens the opportunity to exercise their own religion in Jerusalem.

The foreign sanctuaries erected by Solomon subsisted to the days of Josiah but it is improbable that they were frequented to any considerable extent by native Judaeans. The temple of Astarte was doubtless used by the Phoenician colony which, as we know from Zeph. 1.11, had its quarters in a suburb of the city, and the other temples in like manner would serve for Moabites and Ammonites settled in Jerusalem.[4] At a later date the worship of Melqart, the Baal of Tyre, was introduced into Samaria by Ahab on his marriage with the Tyrian princess Jezebel, whose father Ithobaal was priest of Astarte before he was King of Tyre. Ahab certainly did not forsake the national worship of Jehovah; but on the other hand he plainly designed something more than to provide a private chapel for his wife's use, for at the time of Jehu there were in the Northern Kingdom a number of professed worshippers of Baal, and one of the fruits of the alliance of the Judaean kings with the house of Omri was that a house of Baal was erected also in Jerusalem. In both kingdoms the introduction of a foreign worship was certainly connected with a policy of close alliance with Tyre and in both the innovation proved unsuccessful, not merely on account of the opposition of the prophets in Northern Israel and the priests of the temple at Jerusalem, but because the people at large disliked the foreign ritual and its foreign priests. The revolutions led by Jehu and Jehoiada were supported by popular feeling and in each case one of the first acts of the new government was to put down the worship of Melqart and destroy his temples.

One sees that though the mass of the Israelites were prone to idolatry and readily accepted all the corruptions of Canaanite heathenism if they were disguised under the name of Jehovah worship, they were little disposed to tolerate a foreign god side by side with Jehovah. When Elijah preached that Jehovah is a jealous god and admits no rival in his

---

4.   Cf. Deut. 23.4 (ET 3), which implies that in the seventh century BC there were people of these two nations that had been settled in Judah for many generations and might desire to be admitted to a share in the national worship. Is it because they kept up their own worship at the same time that the Deuteronomic project of law treats them more severely than the Edomites, who had no sanctuary in Jerusalem and in the course of generations might be expected to become good Jehovah worshippers? That the Hebrew Moloch worship was not Malkam-worship seems to be well made out. Cf. W. R. Smith, 'Moloch' in *Encyclopaedia Britannica* XVI (Edinburgh: A. & C. Black, 9th edn, 1883), pp. 695-96.

land his words must have found ready acceptance with many whose own faith in Jehovah was very crass and unenlightened, for indeed the doctrine of divine jealousy may be held in a sense that has nothing to do with spiritual religion and would be as applicable to Chemosh as to Jehovah. That the national god will not tolerate a foreign rival within his land is a natural enough deduction from the old Semitic conception of the god as king of the nation, a deduction that could not fail to be drawn wherever there was a strong spirit of national exclusiveness and jealous dislike of foreigners.

From the time of Elisha onwards the main task of the spiritual prophets was not to banish foreign gods but to purify the worship of Jehovah, and their most effective argument was that in substance, though not in name, the worship of the high places was a worship of strange gods. They felt that their cause was gained if they could convince the people of this; for then they would have the popular conviction on their side as in the days of Elisha and Jehu. It was only in the last days of the kingdom, when the confidence of the nation in itself and its God had been shaken by defeat and servitude to Assyria, that the worship of foreign gods side by side with Jehovah became a serious danger to religion, and so far as we can judge it was again the kings and the ruling classes who were foremost in the service of strange gods. At this time we find evidence of the adoption at Jerusalem of Phoenician rites such as the mourning for Tammuz (Ezek. 8.14), which the Jewish women would take up from the Phoenician colony in the Maktesh (Zeph. 1.11), and Zeph. 1.5 speaks of men who swore by Malkam as well as by Jehovah and who therefore presumably frequented the Ammonite chapel as well as the temple of Jehovah. These were the fruits of Solomon's evil policy; but the main feature in the new idolatries of the Assyrian period was the worship of astral deities, the sun and all the host of heaven. To this worship, which had a great influence on all the later developments of Semitic religion, I shall have to return by and by.

Meantime, we may draw some lessons from the Hebrew which will help us to understand the growth of polytheistic cults in other parts of the Semitic field. The first temples of strange gods in the land of Israel were mainly used by foreign settlers and had a foreign priesthood. And the most important of them were Solomon's temple of the Sidonian Astarte and Ahab's temple of Melqart. Take with this the well-known fact that Solomon was in all things an imitator of Tyre and one may safely conclude that it was the habit of the Phoenicians to encourage foreign merchants to settle in their midst by allowing them to have chapels for their foreign gods. Foreigners in this connection will mean, primarily, men from other Phoenician cities. We know that whenever a Phoenician factory was established across the sea, the settlers took their gods with them and we may be sure that the merchants of Sidon (let us say), who were settled at Tyre, would in like manner desire to have their own chapel. Merchant communities were always great temple builders in antiquity as they are great supporters of churches now, and a rich city like Tyre, which drew settlers from all parts of the Phoenician coast, would soon be enriched with a variety of temples, or rather chapels, of merchant guilds in addition to the original civic sanctuaries. In a cosmopolitan trading city these foreign cults could not give the same offence as the temple of Baal did in Israel; moreover, the Phoenicians were all of one race, had a similar civilization, and doubtless intermarried freely; so that in process of time the chapels would gain general recognition and become public temples open to the whole city, but without prejudice to the special prerogatives of the old civic worship of the king of the city and the goddess associated with him. Our records are too scanty to allow this conjectural account to be verified in every detail; but it agrees with all we know and explains how in later times we find a considerable number of gods that seem to have been acknowledged by all Phoenicians, although each city had a great god or goddess as its special sovereign and protector.[5]

So much for the Phoenicians. But, when we pass from them to the inland peoples where commerce with its tendency to cosmopolitanism was less developed and where there was a high degree of national pride and national exclusiveness, we may infer from the examples supplied by Hebrew history that the obstacles to the formation of an extended national pantheon would be very great. And even where long alliance or complete political union ultimately broke down the jealousy that separated two communities, it would by no means follow with certainty that the united nation would recognize two Baals and worship them side by side. One local god was so like another, both in character and in

5. Work out Tyre (a) with reference to temples: Menander, Herod, temple of Apollo at time of Alexander; (b) with reference to proper names and ask if the families of divine descent from whom kings had to be chosen (see Gutschmid) represent definite city gods. E.g. is the Astarte in the names of Hiram's family Tyrian or Sidonian? Analyse old names in other inscriptions to find several gods worshipped in one family, etc.

ritual, that when their people were united their gods were very apt to be identified, just as all the local Baalim of Israel were regarded as mere local forms of Jehovah. When Jer. 2.28 says that the Judaeans had as many gods as they had cities, he speaks as a prophet to whom an idol has nothing in common with Jehovah; but to the people all the local idols were images of Jehovah as lord of a particular sanctuary. And so it was among the neighbouring peoples also. Among the Philistines, for example, the great temple of Ashdod was dedicated to Dagon (1 Sam. 5; 1 Macc. 10.83); so was that of Gaza (Judg. 16.21-23) and the place names Beth-Dagon and Caphar-Dagon[6] show that the same god was the local Baal of various smaller towns. In Roman times the Philistine cities had a very varied pantheon; in the last days of heathenism, according to Marcus Diaconus,[7] there were eight public temples in Gaza alone. But in biblical times we hear of but one Philistine goddess, Astarte, and of two gods, the national Dagon and the Baal-Zebub of Ekron. And as Baal-Zebub is a *title*, not a *name*, it is very possible that he too was looked upon merely as a local form of Dagon.

Many writers, of whom I name Baethgen as one of the latest,[8] seem to me greatly to exaggerate the polytheism of the nations round about Israel. They seem to take it for granted that, when the Bible speaks of Chemosh, the god of the Moabites, or Malkam, the god of the Ammonites, this only means the chief god out of many. But for this view, which is a clear departure from the natural sense of the biblical expression, I am unable to find justification. Let us look at one or two cases in point.

Among the Moabites, Baethgen[9] thinks he has found evidence of the worship of four gods. Of these the first is, of course, Chemosh and the second is Ashtar-Chemosh, to whose service Mesha consecrated the women and maidens captured by him from the Israelites. A female deity, therefore, is probably meant and the name Ashtar-Chemosh may be interpreted to mean the Ishtar or Astarte who was Chemosh's female partner. Thus far we have only a god and an associated goddess. Then we have Baal-Peor, that is the Baal of Mt Peor, who is taken to be a

6.   P.A.H. de Lagarde, *Onomastica Sacra* (Göttingen: A. Rente, 1870), p. 235 (104, 14).

7.   Marcus Diaconus, *The Life of Porphyry Bishop of Gaza*, p. 64.

8.   F. Baethgen, *Beiträge zur semitischen Religionsgeschichte* (Berlin: H. Reuther, 1888), pp. 9-16.

9.   Baethgen, *Beiträge*, pp. 13-15.

Moabite god, because in the present context of Num. 25.1-3 the corrupt worship of Baal-Peor into which the Israelites were seduced by the Midianites (vv. 14, 18) is mentioned immediately after the idolatry into which they were led by the women of Moab. But this argument is not conclusive, especially as it is probable on critical grounds that the verses that speak of Moabite seductions and those which speak of Baal-Peor come from different sources. Moreover, as 'the Baal of Peor' is a mere title, the more obvious opinion, granting him to be a Moabite deity, is that of Jerome,[10] who identifies him with Chemosh. 'But', says Baethgen,[11] 'Chemosh and Baal-Peor cannot be identical, for while the former is the destroying war god, the latter seems to have been rather a god of fertility and luxury, though no weight can be laid on the Rabbinic fables about his nature and ritual.' Very good, but if the Rabbinic fables are given up, where is the evidence for this contrast between Chemosh and Baal-Peor?—Simply the unchaste rites of his worship. But surely Jehovah of hosts was as much a war god as Chemosh, and yet at every sanctuary of Northern Israel in the time of Hosea his worship was accompanied by prostitution. And does Professor Baethgen suppose that the Hebrew women and maidens consecrated to Ashtar-Chemosh were consecrated to a chaste life?[12] So much for the third Moabite god. The fourth is a pure creature of fancy. 'Mt Nebo' says Baethgen,[13] 'can only have its name from the Babylonian God Nebo and must have been sacred to him.' By no means, for as Nöldeke observes, Nebo may simply mean 'the height' (Arabic, *an-nabāwah*).[14]

As regards the Ammonites, Baethgen admits[15] that there is no evidence that they worshipped any god but Malkam and perhaps Astarte. For Edomite worship before the captivity we have only the evidence of

10. J.-P. Migne, *Patrologiae cursus completus. Series Latina* XXIV (Paris, J.-P. Migne, 1845), col. 168 (= 185). 'In Nabo enim erat Chamos idolum consecratum quod alio nomine appellatur Baalphegor.'

11. Baethgen, *Beiträge*, p. 15. [ET by W.R.S.]

12. To argue from the symbols on the signet of Kemoshyehi (C.J.M. de Vogüé, *Mélanges d'archéologie orientale* [Paris: Imprimerie Impériale, 1868], p. 89) that Chemosh is a solar god is not admissible. The winged disc is the general Assyrian symbol of deity and proves nothing except that the seal was cut in the period of Assyrian influence.

13. Baethgen, *Beiträge*, p. 15. [ET by W.R.S.]

14. Nöldeke, review of Baethgen's *Beiträge zur semitischen Religionsgeschichte*, p. 470.

15. Baethgen, *Beiträge*, p. 15.

proper names, which leave us in some doubt whether the Edomites had a common national god at all—none such is mentioned in the Old Testament—and all we know about these wild mountaineers is consistent with the supposition that the various tribes continued to have distinct religions. In Damascus, on the other hand, we find at least two gods, Hadad and Rimmon, which seem to have been fused together as Hadad-Rimmon (Zech. 12.11).[16]

While it thus appears that the growth of an extensive practical polytheism among the northern Semites was but slow and that national feeling, where it was strong, tended to make the acknowledged gods fewer rather than to multiply them, it would be a great mistake to ascribe to the national religions any real tendency towards monotheism. Everywhere except in Israel the loss of national independence led to a great spread of polytheism and a free adoption of foreign gods.

Here then we come to the third point of comparison with the Greek system and have to ask whether among the Semites, where several gods were worshipped together, the plurality of cults was justified by ascribing to each god a distinctive character and a separate function. It is often assumed as a matter of course that this must have been the case, apparently for no better reason than that it was so in Greece and that differentiation of function is the easiest and most obvious explanation of the existence of practical polytheism. But in dealing with times and manners remote from our own nothing is so unsafe as to assume a probability in favour of what seems easy and natural to us. A somewhat better argument may be sought in the observation that the Greeks in Asia thought that they recognized a substantial identity between certain Hellenic and Semitic deities and that the Semites accepted these identifications. Thus among the Phoenician deities Melqart was identified with Heracles, Astarte with Aphrodite, Resheph with Apollo, Eshmun with Asklepios, El with Kronos, and so forth, and this, it may be urged, goes to show that these Phoenician deities were differentiated from each other in much the way as the corresponding gods of Greece. But a little consideration will show that the force of this argument is extremely limited. The oldest and most solid of the identifications, namely that of Aphrodite and Astarte, applies to a goddess whom the Greeks borrowed

---

16. I.e. if Rimmon is a god = *R'mn* and not a goddess. E. Schrader, 'Assyrisch-babylonisches. 3.', *Jahrbücher für protestantische Theologie* 1 (1875), pp. 334-38 and *Die Keilinschriften und das Alte Testament*, pp. 205-206 and Baethgen, *Beiträge*, p. 75 are not quite convincing.

from the Semites and the specialization of function that made her the goddess of love seems to have taken place after she was borrowed. The name of Astarte (pl. Ashtaroth) is derived from the Babylonian Ishtar, but it was through the Phoenicians or maritime Canaanites that she reached Greece. In Canaanite religion Astarte is a name almost as wide in its significance as Baal. In the Old Testament the Baalim and the Ashtaroth, that is, the Baals and the Astartes, is the general designation of the divine pairs that were worshipped side by side in the local sanctuaries (Judg. 10.6; 1 Sam. 7.4, 12.10) where, as we have seen, the god and his partner were of a highly generalized type and concerned themselves with all the wants of their worshippers. But as was shown in the first course of these lectures, the sacred feasts of the Canaanites are connected with the seasons of agriculture and this means that the chief gift sought of the gods was the gift of *fertility* to the soil, to the flocks and herds and also, of course, to the human species. The local Baal and his spouse were worshipped especially at the seasons of natural increase and conceived above all things as productive powers.

If now we bear in mind that the Semites are by nature prone to sensuality and habitually take a somewhat crude view of marriage and of the relations of the sexes generally, we can see that Astarte as the spouse of the Baal, the female element in the divine energy of production and reproduction, could not fail to assume a sensual type, and that in her images and worship the mere physical side of womanhood and mother-hood would be accentuated, rather than the ideal of the 'ewig Weibliche', which has had so potent and ennobling an influence on our Western civilization. Accordingly, the Canaanite worship of Astarte was habitually associated with religious prostitution, and the grossness of her nude terracotta images found in Cyprus is quite in keeping with the vileness of her rites. It was from the Phoenician colonies of Cyprus and Cythera that the worship of the oriental Aphrodite spread through Greece and the nature of her rites, as contrasted with the native Hellenic cults, at once marked her out as the goddess of sensual love. But on Semitic soil there was no contrast between Astarte-worship and the rites of other deities which could serve to distinguish her as specifically the goddess of love. Wherever, in the north Semitic area, we find an important cult of a female deity, we find the same sensual ideas and practices, for these practices did not spring out of anything peculiar to Astarte but out of the general character of the religious life of the race. The goddesses differ from one another in their names and titles and in some superficial character, but the general type is always the same. At Byblos, for example, the goddess is not called Astarte, but goes by the title of the 'Lady the Baalath of Gebal', Graecized by Philo of Byblos as Baaltis.[17] But to all effects and purposes she is simply the local Astarte, worshipped with the same sensuous rites and associated with the myth and orgies of Adonis. Accordingly, she also is taken by Lucian[18] to be Aphrodite, though Philo makes her Dione, and Plutarch identifies her with Isis.[19]

In none of these forms is the great Semitic goddess properly described as the goddess of love and fecundity in the sense in which Aphrodite may be so described. She still remains a goddess of universal powers and functions. To bring this out, let us consider what a man had to ask of his god in addition to those gifts of natural fecundity which we have already been considering. Three things pretty well fill up the circle, namely counsel in perplexity, help against enemies and long life. Now we know that Astarte and the kindred goddesses of the Semites granted oracles, for example at Aphaca and at Paphos.[20] They had prophets and prophetesses[21] and revealed themselves also in dreams (Assyrian Ishtar). Again, that the goddess had a martial aspect and was invoked to help her people in war appears from much evidence. In Assyria Ishtar is above all things a warlike goddess in accordance with the military character of the state. Among the small agricultural communities of inland Syria or the trading cities of the Phoenician coast this side of her character is naturally less prominent. But at Ascalon the Philistines consecrate the armour of Saul in the temple of Astarte (1 Sam. 31.10), which implies that her help was acknowledged in connection with the

---

17. *CIS* 1.1. Syriac *Bel(a)thi*, in Melito, 'Oration', in Cureton, *Spicilegium Syriacum*, p. 44 (= Syriac, p. 45).

18. *De Dea Syria*, 6.

19. On the stele of Byblos she has the Egyptian headdress with uraeus, disc and moon's horns. This connects her with Isis-Hathor but also with the Sidonian Astarte whom Lucian (*De Dea Syria*, 4) takes to be the Moon. This is ultimately the bull's head of Astarte in Philo of Byblos, fragment 24. When Plutarch calls the queen of Byblos Astarte, wife of Malkandros, he really implies that the goddess was so named (*Isis and Osiris*, 15).

20. Our accounts of the oracle refer to Titus's visit, but the oracle was of Phoenician origin and administered by priests who claimed Phoenician descent.

21. E.g. at Carthage: A. Bouché-Leclercq, *L'histoire de la Divination dans l'antiquité* III (Paris: E. Leroux, 1880), p. 410. Cf. the prophets of the Asherah in 1 Kgs 18.19.

victory over Israel, and with this it agrees that Aphrodite was represented by an armed statue in the sanctuary of Cythera, the oldest in
Greece, where the cultus was directly borrowed from the Phoenicians,
and according to Herodotus (1.105) from the region of Ascalon, and
that in Cyprus also we find an *Encheios Aphroditē* (Hesychius,
Lexicon). The Tyche or city goddess of Laodicea ad Mare is represented
armed on coins of the Roman empire, and from this attribute she is
identified by the Greeks sometimes with Pallas, sometimes with the
Brauronian Artemis.[22] She is, of course, in reality only one of the many
local Ashtaroth. We find the king of Byblos praying to her to bless him
and give him life and prolong his days over Byblos and grant him
favour in the eyes of the gods and the people. So much for Astarte, who
is evidently a goddess of the most generalized type and so might be
identified by a Greek with almost any one of his own goddesses
according to the particular aspect of her multiform character in which
she happened to be presented to him.

And all the Semitic goddesses are of this highly generalized type. Take,
for example, the great goddess of Hierapolis in Syria, whom Lucian calls
Hera but who is really Atargatis, that is an Aramaic modification of the
ubiquitous Astarte connected with the god Athe. Her statue, says
Lucian, declares her to be a goddess with a great variety of characters.
'On the whole she is undoubtedly Hera, but she has something of
Athena, of Aphrodite, of the Moon-goddess, of Rhea, of Artemis, of
Nemesis, and of the Fates' (*De Dea Syria*, 32). Evidently the Syrian
artist had heaped on the goddess every symbol that could emphasize the
comprehensive character of her power and attributes.[23]

22. Smith, *Religion of the Semites* (1st series, 1st edn), p. 447 (= 2nd edn,
pp. 466-67).

23. For Tanith = Artemis we have no information to lead us to think her a more
specialized goddess. And *'nt* with epithet *ēz ḥayyîm = Athēnai Sōteirai* (*CIS* 1.95), on
whom C.J.M. de Vogüé has written ('Inscriptions phéniciennes de l'île de Cypre',
Journal Asiatique 10 [1867], pp. 120-29, 157-60), is only known by her identification
with the Egyptian Anata (which will be here meant, as a king Ptolemy is referred to).
She can hardly therefore be built on, though if she is Anaitis she is, as I have shown
(cf. W.R. Smith, 'Semiramis', in *Encyclopaedia Britannica* XXI [Edinburgh:
A. & C. Black, 9th edn, 1886], pp. 639-40, and 'Ctesias and the Semiramis Legend',
English Historical Review 2.6 [April, 1887], pp. 303-17) essentially = Astarte. On
Anath: against her Assyrian origin but for the view that she is Hittite, see E. Meyer,
'Ueber einige semitische Götter', *ZDMG* 31 (1877), pp. 716-41. Gad = Tyche is not
a name but a title (of a local Astarte). The fates (*Manāt, et al.*) are, I suspect, the same.

So far as I can make out, every Semitic goddess concentrated in herself all possible divine characters and functions. The chief visible difference between one goddess and another was that in one place the local female deity was associated with a husband, in another with a son, in a third she was worshipped alone as if unmarried. In the first case she might be taken to be Hera, in the second to be Rhea, in the third to be Artemis, or Athena, but these identifications were purely arbitrary and throw no light on the real character of the divinity.

The Greeks were not more happy in their attempts to find Hellenic gods among the male deities of the Semites. In most cases it is impossible to say why a particular identification was pitched on, but it is probable that the reasons often lay in some trait of ritual, as when Plutarch and others concluded from the rites of the feast of Tabernacles that Bacchus was worshipped by the Jews.[24] The example shows the worthlessness of all such inferences.

The Greek identifications show that the services, the divine symbols, or the sacred myths which they found at Eastern sanctuaries reminded them of features in their own religion. They prove that in these respects Semitic worship was not absolutely uniform and colourless: it would indeed be strange if it had been so; but they are not good evidence for ascribing to any Semitic deity a differentiated character corresponding to that of his supposed Hellenic equivalent. For example, it is quite unsafe to argue, as is done by so recent a writer as Baethgen,[25] that the Phoenician Eshmun was god of healing because the Greeks identify him with Asklepios.

I will examine the case somewhat fully, because it is much relied on and has produced an impression even on Pietschmann, who has argued with great force in his recent *History of Phoenicia*[26] that all the Phoenician gods are originally local or tribal and therefore of a highly generalized type. This is the very view for which I have been arguing, but in the case of Eshmun, Pietschmann yet believes that at Berytus in

---

Note that in the Nabataean inscriptions *mnwtw* appears as a *triptote*. So, no doubt, do names of the form *ymlkw*. The *manāyā* are not thoroughly personified. Arabic goddesses are certainly not differentiated. Who can distinguish Al-Lāt from Al-'Ozzā? The forms, like the Kore of Elusa, belong to the subject of married and unmarried goddesses.

24. Plutarch, *Symposiaca* 4.Q.5, cf. Tacitus, *The Histories*, 5.5.

25. Baethgen, *Beiträge*, p. 44.

26. Pietschmann, *Geschichte der Phönizier*, pp. 170-74.

the Greek period the main function of the god was to heal sickness, 'though in all probability this was only one of the many functions originally ascribed to him'.[27] I maintain on the contrary that Eshmun was a great Baal with the same circle of kingly functions that belong to any other great local Baal, that one of these functions was healing, but that this does not distinguish him from other deities and that there is no evidence that the art of healing was specially ascribed to him.

The oldest seats of the worship of Eshmun appear to be Sidon and Berytus. The river of Sidon, now the Nahr Barghūt, was called by the Greeks the Asklepios, and at its source most probably lay the temple in the mountain beside a fountain which King Eshmunazar of Sidon built to the god whose name he bore. The gods specially worshipped by the dynasty of Eshmunazar were Eshmun and Astarte and to both of these the king built temples, to one in the mountain, to the other at the coast. He also built a pair of temples in Sidon to the gods of the Sidonians 'to the Baal of Sidon and to Astarte, name of Baal (*šēm ba'al*)'.

It has been proposed to distinguish between the divine pair worshipped by the royal family and the Baal and Astarte of the town. But it is far more probable that the Baal of Sidon, of whom we hear only in this passage and in the new Piraeus inscription, is Eshmun in his quality of god of the City. The whole valley of the Asklepios, like the valley of the Adonis, would naturally have one Baal, and the king would hardly bear the name of any other than the chief god of his people. That the Eshmun of Sidon was the supreme god is, I think, made probable by another circumstance. Renan found in the environs of Cyprus an inscription of the second Christian century[28] recording how *Threptiōn (N)eikōnos tou Sōsippou tous duo leontas Dii oreiōi, kat' onar, ek tōn idiōn, eurebōn anethēken.* The mountain Zeus at Sidon can hardly be any other god than the Eshmun whose mountain sanctuary Eshmunazar built, and Zeus is necessarily the supreme god. And that the great god of the Sidonian mountain is Eshmun and no one else may be argued from the lions dedicated to him.

These two lions may be compared with the two golden gazelles in the Well Zemzem and the two golden camels dedicated to Dhu Samāi on a Himyaritic inscription and to Dusares in a Nabataean inscription of

---

27. Pietschmann, *Geschichte der Phönizier*, p. 187. [ET by W.R.S.]
28. Renan, *Mission de Phénicie*, p. 397.

Puteoli.[29] They imply that there was some connection between the god and the lion. Now according to Marinus[30] *Asklēpios leontouchos* appears at Ascalon and from the context appears to be the chief god there worshipped.[31] At Carthage the temple of Asklepios occupied the summit of the citadel hill and was by far the most splendid in the town.[32] That the Asklepios of Appian is Eshmun is generally accepted and confirmed by *CIS* 1.252, where the temple of Eshmun is mentioned. His temple also held a chief place at New Carthage[33] so that he is evidently one of the greatest Carthaginian gods. And here, as at Sidon, he is associated with Astarte, as the compound form shows.[34] At Citium in Cyprus he is worshipped as Eshmun-Melqart. As such he may perhaps have been identified with the Tyrian Heracles (and this suggests that in Hannibal's oath [Polybius, 7.9] Heracles may be Eshmun, for Melqart and Astarte are a pair and so are Eshmun and Astarte); at all events the name shows that he was king of the city, the great local Baal. Finally, to pass over other traces of his worship, Eshmun was a great god at Berytus and here the legend recorded that he was a beautiful and youthful huntsman who was pursued by the love of Astronoe, the mother of the gods, a form of Astarte. To escape from her he inflicted on himself a terrible—apparently a fatal—mutilation, but was restored by the goddess and made a god.[35] This is a very late legend and cannot be trusted in detail but it is evidently only one of the many forms of the

29. T. Nöldeke, 'Zwei goldene Kameele als Votivgeschenke bei Arabern', *ZDMG* 38 (1884), pp. 143-44.

30. Marinus, *Vita Procli*, p. 19.

31. The force of this argument is perhaps weakened by the existence of other lion gods like the *Gennaios* of Heliopolis. See Smith, *Religion of the Semites* (1st series, 1st edn), p. 156 (= 2nd edn, pp. 444-45). If the Baal of Sidon has the lion as the Astarte sits on the bull, this is the exact opposite of Heliopolis, where the goddess sits on the lion and the god on the bull. At any rate *gd b'l* = Leontopodion (in Africa) shows that the lion-god is Baal. All this makes Eshmun rather the lion-killing Heracles of the patera (Pietschmann, *Geschichte der Phönizier*, p. 189) than the cherub-slaying youth (Iolaos!). Cf. also the lion of the Colossus of Amathus (G. Perrot and C. Chipiez, *Histoire de l'Art* III (Paris: Hachette, 1885), p. 567 and the two lions (*'rwm*) dedicated to Resheph-Ḥēṣ (*CIS* 1.10, line 3).

32. Appian, *Roman History*, 8.130.

33. Polybius, 10.10.8.

34. *CIS* 1.245.

35. The text of Damascius, *Life of Isidore*, 302, is rendered 'summoning Paion the divine Physician' rather than 'calling the youth Paion'. Read *te tēi* for *tēi te*?

story of Adonis, with the special features which the myth of the death and resurrection of the god assumes where there is a priesthood of Eunuchs.[36] In all this there is nothing to support the view that Eshmun was a god of specialized gifts and limited power. He is a Baal of the usual regal type, and like other great Baals he is associated with Astarte and is a huntsman god conquering lions. All the few traits of legend associated with him belong to Baal myths in general. So great a god cannot but have the power of healing, especially where he is associated with a sacred stream, for all Semitic holy waters have healing power. Accordingly in a famous trilingual inscription of Sardinia (*CIS* 1.143) we find a votive altar erected to Eshmun-Mearreh[37] by a man whom he had healed.[38] But this gives us no right to make him a healing god in any distinctive sense. Even in late Phoenician mythology, when the Euhemerists were eager to ascribe special discoveries useful to man to particular gods, it is not Eshmun who discovers healing drugs and spells, but a later generation of deities, the sons of his brethren the Cabiri.[39]

I will not weary you with the arguments by which the school of Movers have tried to make out the halting thesis that Eshmun is really the god of healing.[40] But I will notice one curious point which seems to show that, like other Baals, he was a god of *prophecy*. A form of Solanum mentioned by Dioscorides was called, in the Punic tongue, Eshmun's herb. Now the Solanum produces frenzy and another species of it is known from Pliny to have been used to produce mantic excitement.[41] With this it agrees that, according to Apuleius, the same

36. Cf. Attis, and Combabus at Hierapolis. In Lucian's story an historical personage, Stratonice, wife of Seleucus, is worked in (Strato for Astarte?). It is clear from ch. 26 that Lucian has rationalized the story and that Combabus was originally the beloved of Hera = Atargatis. Cf. the similar rites in the worship of Tar'atha at Edessa (Bardesan, 'Book of the laws of countries', in Cureton, *Spicilegium Syriacum*, p. 40 [= Syriac, p. 31]).

37. *CIS* 1.143. 'Wanderer' or 'conductor'? Nöldeke, review of F. Baethgen, *Beiträge zur semitischen Religionsgeschichte*, pp. 470-87. Cf. p. 472, where he refers to Eshmun. It is a trilingual inscription from Pauli Gerrei.

38. It is possible that *B'l mrp'* at Citium (*CIS* 1.41) is also Eshmun and that the Greeks got the identification thence.

39. 'Philo of Byblos', in J.C. von Orelli, *Sanchoniathonis Berytii quae feruntur fragmenta de Cosmogonia et Theologia Phoenicum* (Leipzig: Hinrichs, 1826), p. 24.

40. F.K. Movers, *Die Phönizier* I (Bonn: E. Weber, 1841), pp. 533-34.

41. Be warned against attending to rubbish about Eshmun being air with which a Phoenician tried to gull Pausanias (Pausanias, *Description of Greece*, 7.23.8).

herb which the Phoenicians named after Eshmun was called Apollinaris in Italy, after the god of Prophecy. Eshmun therefore was a prophetic god with frenzied diviners as his priests.[42]

42. See at length in S. Bochart, *Geographia Sacra seu Phaleg et Canaan* (Leiden: C. Bontesteyn & J. Luchtmans, 4th edn, 1707), lib. II, cap. XV, col. 760.

Third Series, Lecture 3

THE GODS AND THE WORLD: COSMOGONY

'The origin of the world and of man' says Lang,[1] 'is naturally a problem which has excited the curiosity of the least developed minds. Every savage race has its own myths on the subject, all of them bearing the marks of the childish and crude imagination' characteristic of early races

> and all varying in amount of what may be called philosophical thought...
> All the cosmogonic myths waver between the theory of construction, or
> rather of reconstruction, and the theory of evolution, very rudely conceived.
> The earth, as a rule, is thought to have grown out of some original matter,
> perhaps an animal, perhaps an egg which floated on the waters, perhaps a
> handful of mud from below the waters... The ages before the development
> or creation of man are filled up, in the myths, with the loves and wars of
> supernatural people

—often gigantic monsters, half-human, half-bestial, and not generally immortal.

> The appearance of man is explained in three or four contradictory ways,
> each of which is represented in the various legends of most mythologies.
> Sometimes man is fashioned out of clay, or stone, or other materials, by
> one of the older species of beings, half-human or bestial, but also half-
> divine. Sometimes the first man rises out of the earth and is himself
> confused with the creator... Sometimes man arrives ready made, with most
> of the animals, from his former home in a hole in the ground, and he
> furnishes the world for himself with stars, sun, moon, and everything else
> he needs. Again, there are many myths which declare that man was evolved
> out of one or other of the lower animals [or he] is taken to be the fruit of
> some tree or plant, or...to have grown out of the ground like a plant...
> Lastly, man is occasionally represented as having been framed out of a
> piece of the body of the creator, or made by some demiurgic potter out of
> clay. All these legends are told by savages, with no sense of their

1.   A. Lang, *Myth, Ritual, and Religion* I (London: Longmans, Green, 1887), pp. 165-67.

inconsistency. There is no single orthodoxy in the matter, and...all these
theories coexist pell-mell among the mythological traditions of civilised
races.

These general remarks on early cosmogonies will be useful to us in
looking specially at the fragments of Semitic cosmogonies that have
come down to us. They may serve to warn us against seeking too much,
against the attempt to build up out of the Babylonian and Phoenician
records a single consistent picture of the origin of the universe and of
man. This warning is not necessary when we approach the subject, as
most of us do, from the side of the Old Testament. The simple and
grand cosmogony of Genesis 1 has no parallel among the heathen
Semites because none of them has such a conception of God the creator.
We shall see as we proceed that the pictorial details of the Hebrew story
of creation bear a certain resemblance to the details of other, and
notably of Babylonian creation myths. But the resemblance has been
greatly exaggerated and the unity of the story in which the whole
creation appears as one progressive and well-ordered work of God is not
borrowed from Babylon, while the lesson of the story which makes it fit
to stand at the head of the record of Revelation and Redemption is
entirely foreign to Semitic heathenism.

In the Old Testament the doctrine of one God the creator of all is one
of the chief cornerstones of practical religion. Among the heathen the
origin of the world is a matter of mere curiosity, which is discussed in a
fluctuating and uncertain body of myths. The gods enter into these
myths, for they are themselves part of the universe of things; but what
they did and suffered in the cosmogonic age is practically unimportant
for religion. If the cosmogonic myths had been wholly wiped out,
Semitic heathenism would still have stood just where it was. But where
would the religion of the Bible be without God the maker of all?

In a complete cosmogony we should expect to find three main topics
treated: (a) the origin of heaven and earth, (b) the origin of the gods, (c)
the origin of man. But we must not expect to find all these topics
embraced in every cosmogonic myth. Among the Arabs, for example, I
have not found any trace of a myth of the origin of heaven and earth;
these seem to be taken for granted as facts about which it is needless to
speculate.

Again, as regards the origin of the gods, all the Semites think of the
gods as begetting and begotten and must therefore have had rudiments
of a theogony. But how the first and oldest gods, the parents of the

divine race, came to be is a further question to which we cannot generally find an answer and which many Semites probably never put to themselves.

Finally, as regards the origin of man we shall not always find a theory of the origin of mankind as a whole but only special theories held in individual tribes as regards their own origin—as when one Arab tribe is born of rocks, another of a *si'lāt* (female demon), a third are children of the sun, etc. And in general it may be remarked that cosmogonic myths do not generally spring from any wide view of the universe but are evidently local stories invented in a narrow circle to account for its own existence and surroundings. For example, the Demiurge is usually the city God and the creator is also the builder of the city.

For the cosmogonies of the Semites we are practically limited to Babylonian and Phoenician sources. The Babylonian account of the beginning of the world is partly preserved in the so-called Creation tablets now in the British Museum. These tablets, which are Assyrian copies of Babylonian originals, belonged to the library of Asshurbanipal, who came to the throne in 668 BC, that is they were written about a generation after Isaiah prophesied. The story they contain is, of course, very much older and is the most ancient cosmogony in the world. The Babylonian fragments are very imperfect and often hard to understand. Fortunately, we can compare them with two accounts of the Babylonian cosmogony preserved in Greek. One of these, which we owe to the Greek philosopher Damascius, covers the same ground as the first Creation tablet and helps to fill up its blanks. The other account, which is that of Berosus, has reached us by a somewhat complicated path through Alexander Polyhistor, Eusebius and George Syncellus. It also gives substantially the same cosmogony as the tablets, but very much abridged. Putting all these sources together we can form a tolerably clear and certain account of the Babylonian legend. Without Damascius and Berosus the fragmentary tablets would hardly have been intelligible.

Our knowledge of the Phoenician cosmogonies is again due to Damascius and Eusebius, especially to the long extracts given by the latter from the writings of Philo of Byblos. Philo was a Hellenized Phoenician, full of theories, whose special object was to show that all the myths of the gods are histories of mortal men deified after their death for the benefits they conferred on mankind. In the service of this theory he gathered together a number of the myths current at Byblos and other Phoenician cities and tried to work them into a kind of continuous history. That the myths suffered a good deal in this rationalizing process may be safely assumed; and they have suffered a further mutilation at the hands of Eusebius, who quotes them only so far as they serve his argument against heathenism and in favour of Christianity. To get anything like complete order out of the fragments is now impossible and some parts are almost quite unintelligible. But there is no doubt that they contain a great deal of genuine Phoenician legend mixed up with later speculation. The legends and speculations, moreover, are so entirely the product of very divergent habits of mind that we can often separate them with certainty.

A. *The Babylonian Creation Story*

The Hebrew account of the creation bears the title, 'These are the generations of the heavens and the earth' (Gen. 2.4) and is summed up in the words of 2.1, 'Thus the heavens and the earth were finished, and all the host of them.' In like manner the generations of the heavens and the earth, or the making of heaven and earth and their denizens, would fairly sum up the contents of the Babylonian creation legend. By the heavens the Babylonians, like the Hebrews, understand the visible firmament, the dome which is spread out over the habitable earth 'like a curtain...like a tent to dwell in' (Isa. 40.22). To both nations the dome of heaven is a solid sphere (*rāqî'a*) on which the heavenly bodies move. Beyond this dome are waters,[2] which would fall on the earth and submerge it, if the windows of heaven were opened.[3] As there are waters above the heavens, so in like manner the earth rests on waters and is bounded on all sides by the circumambient ocean, Apsu.[4] The Apsu also extends beneath the earth,[5] for example as in Ps. 24.2 the earth is founded upon the seas. The cosmos, therefore, in the old Semitic view is an enclosed space between the outspread earth and the domed heaven, surrounded on all sides by an unlimited expanse of water. The problem of creation is to explain how this region, cut off from the dark

2.   Creation tablet 4, 139. 140. Cf. Gen. 1.7, 7.11.

3.   In 2 Kgs 7.2 the windows of heaven are rather those through which God can pour down supernatural gifts. So too in Babylonia and Assyria there is a *kirib šamî* from which the sun comes out (cf. Psalm 19). So Jensen, *Die Kosmologie*, p. 10, but this seems another conception from that of the tablets.

4.   ? = *'epes*, J. Halévy. See Jensen, *Die Kosmologie*, pp. 243-53.

5.   Jensen, *Die Kosmologie*, p. 252.

primordial ocean and instinct with light and life, took its beginning.

The Chaldaean cosmogony assumes that the Apsu (Apason of Damascius) or primordial ocean existed in the beginning, before the gods were shaped, before heaven and earth existed. This ocean was the first father, and the first mother was Tiamat, Tiamtu, Tamat, Tauthe of Damascius,[6] Thalatth, that is Thamte of Berosus, or as she is called in tablet 1, Mumu Tiamat, the seething deep. In ordinary language *tiāmat* means the 'sea', that is the Persian Gulf as distinct from the vast untramelled ocean, but here, as in Gen. 1.2, it has a special meaning,[7] designating the watery chaotic abyss in which primaeval life arose by the mixing of its waters with those of Apsu and out of which heaven and earth were ultimately shaped. Tiamat is the mother of all,[8] the mother of the gods,[9] and this conception the audacious primitive imagination took in a literal way. In Berosus she is a woman presiding over the monsters that swarmed in the dark waters of primordial chaos; in the creation tablets she is a huge animated being, a sort of dragon that makes war with the Demiurge. It is plain from a comparison of the sources that the watery darkness of Berosus, in which monstrous animals that cannot bear light are engendered, is the womb of Tiamat; instead of saying that the First Mother rules over these strange beings compounded of the parts of various animals, it would be more accurate to say that she encircles them. These monsters are the first gods or demigods; the dragons, and bulls with human heads and other wild compound forms, of which, as Berosus says, the images were still to be seen in the temple of Bel—all the strange figures of primitive mythology which can be studied now on the oldest Chaldaean cylinders.[10] But besides this chaotic brood it appears that Tiamat gave birth to the race of gods proper. In

---

6.   In Damascius, *De Principiis* (in C.A.[E.] Ruelle (ed.), *Damascii successoris dubitationes et solutiones de primis principiis* I [Paris: C. Klincksieck, 1889], p. 125) Moymis is the only begotten son of Apason and Tauthe.

7.   In Hebrew (Gen. 7.11) the primaeval waters under the earth are *tᵉhôm*. In Babylon these belong to the Apsu.

8.   Creation tablet 1.4.

9.   Damascius, (see n. 6).

10.   In Damascius (see n. 6) and on Creation tablet 1, these monsters are represented by a simple pair, Dache and Dachos (?Lache, Lachos) = Lachmu and Lachamu. That these are monsters of the type of Berosus is clear from an inscription of Nabonidus (Schrader [ed.], *Keilinschriftliche Bibliothek*, p. 101), where they are set up at the East Gate of a temple to destroy enemies. They are like the wild ox (*ri-i-mu*) mentioned just before, or the bull guardians.

the creation tablets there is a lacuna at this point, but in Damascius she gives birth, after the monsters, to the pair Kissare and Assoros, who in turn bear the three gods Anos, Illinos, and Aos. There is fortunately just enough left of the tablet to tell us that the first pair are An-šar and Kišar, the 'whole upper' and 'whole lower', which we might render heaven and earth, were it not that these are created later. But as Anos is certainly Anu, whose seat is the pole of the heavens, and Aos is certainly Ea, whose special sphere is the sea, we can see the general sense to be that the gods of the upper and lower world alike sprang from the race of Tiamat.

Thus far the conception, if grotesque, is fairly consistent; but now comes a gap in the tablets which the parallel sources do nothing to fill and which seems to involve a contradiction. When the story begins again the real gods, Anu, Ea and their progeny, are at war with Tiamat and ultimately they make an end of her and her monstrous brood. They had escaped somehow from the matrix of chaos, but they had not yet received their seats in heaven, which did not yet exist. Where they were we must not ask; primitive cosmogonies do not bear cross-examination. At all events there was war between the gods and Tiamat, and Marduk, the Bel of Babylon, son of Anu and Daukine,[11] after a terrible fight slays Tiamat and, cutting her in two, makes heaven of one half and the earth of the other.

As regards their substance, therefore, the dome of heaven and the expanse of earth are nothing else than the two halves of the matrix or envelope of the dark seething waters of primaeval chaos, opened up and modelled into a cosmos. The main difference between chaos and cosmos in the story of Berosus (Damascius here deserts us) lies in the breaking in of light when Bel-Marduk clave the darkness. For the monstrous brood of yore could not endure the light but perished, and so a vast fruitful land, the Babylonian alluvium, was left ready to receive a new and higher creation.[12] This feature does not seem to appear in the tablets, but they, on the other hand, attach much importance to the winds as allies of Marduk. They seem to have played their part by blowing down her throat and inflating her interior.

Perhaps, then, we may conclude that air and light conspire to

11. Dauke in Damascius.
12. The tablets do not seem quite to agree with this, for in 4.109 the helpers of Tiamat, which can hardly be other than her monstrous brood, appear to be left alive though imprisoned (banished from earth).

differentiate cosmos from chaos. It is these two elements that fill the space between heaven and earth and make orderly life possible.[13] That life, however, had still to be created, at least as regards the earth; for the host of heaven already existed in the shape of the gods that assisted Marduk in his war and for them it was only necessary to assign their places in the heavens. Accordingly, Berosus tells us that Bel fashioned (*aneplasen*) the stars, the sun, the moon and the seven planets, and the creation tablet describes at length how he made the heavenly bodies and assigned them as posts to the great gods. I ask you to note that in this ancient record the gods and the heavenly bodies are not identified; the latter are only the assigned places of the former.

As regards the earth, since the old monsters that could not bear the light had disappeared, a fresh creation was necessary and this Bel provided by cutting off his own head, or having it cut off, and directing the other gods to mix the blood that streamed forth with dust and make men, or according to another version, men and animals.[14] Such is the Chaldaean cosmogony in its Babylonian form.

I think you will at once admit that the parallelism between it and Genesis 1, on which most recent writers lay stress, has been greatly exaggerated. The main point of agreement is that both accounts begin with a dark chaos. But in the Babylonian legend the chaos is productive and all things are born of it; in the Bible the chaos is only the raw material of creation from which the orderly elements of the cosmos are separated by the creative word of God. Then as regards the steps of the creation I am unable to find any greater parallelism between the two accounts than follows naturally from the fact that Hebrews and Babylonians had similar conceptions of the physical constitution of the universe, for example, the solid expanse of heaven stretched like a dome

13. Cf. the Phoenician in Pausanias, *Description of Greece*, 7.23.8, who makes Asklepios (Eshmun) air, son of Apollo the sun, and the part of sun and wind in vivifying the creation in Philo (Eusebius, *Praep. Ev.*, 33d).

14. K. Budde, *Die biblische Urgeschichte* (Giessen: J. Ricker, 1883), p. 480 will not admit Gutschmid's two sources and will have it that the second account only repeats the first. But the differences are considerable and the second account is not a mere repetition but a softening response, a rationalization. (1) Bel does not cut off his own head; (2) *one* god (not the other gods) does the creation; (3) only men are formed and therefore are rational and partake of the divine intelligence. Surely this is another and later account and may well be Polyhistor as against the Book of Oannes, or rather Berosus himself as against his source.

over the earth. Wellhausen[15] has justly remarked that in Genesis 1 every
step in creation follows in natural order; the whole is clearly thought out,
not borrowed from a previous mythology.[16] Great weight has been laid
on a probable agreement between the Hebrew and Babylonian creation
as regards the order of the works of creation. This, however, is tolerably
uncertain except as regards points in which the order is given by the
necessities of the case. Thus, Jensen[17] points out that the uplifting of
heaven in tablet 4 precedes the separation of land and water. This is not
very clear in the Babylonian text, but plainly it could hardly be
otherwise.[18] On the other hand, some of the most striking features in the
Bible story, for example that the creation of light and the first growth of
plants precede the creation of the heavenly bodies, cannot be shown to
reappear in the Chaldaean myth. In Berosus's story, indeed, the creation
of the heavenly luminaries is mentioned after the death of the animals
that cannot bear the light. But there also is no doubt that Eusebius has
made a transposition here, for he also mentions the creation of men and
beasts before the creation of sun, moon and stars, and this cannot be
right, as we see from the tablets. For the present, at least till the blanks
in the creation story are supplied, we cannot say with certainty that light
shone in the Babylonian chaos before the sun was made.[19] As regards
the creation of plants, of which no record is preserved in the existing
Babylonian sources, it is tolerably clear that, if it was spoken of at all, it
came after the creation of the luminaries.[20] On the other hand, the

15. Wellhausen, *Prolegomena zur Geschichte Israels*, pp. 312-13. (ET
Prolegomena to the History of Israel, pp. 297-98.)

16. There is one feature, 'the spirit of God brooding on the deep', which has no
connection with what follows and may be connected with older ideas. Cf. Ps. 104.30
and Dan. 7.2 with the Phoenician 'wind Colpia' (Eusebius, *Praep. Ev.*, 34b) = *rūaḥ
kol pē'â*.

17. Jensen, *Die Kosmologie*, p. 305 (cf. p. 198).

18. That Belus separated earth and sea seems to be stated (though the text is
corrupt) in a fragment of Abydenus (C. Müller [ed.], *Fragmenta historicorum
Graecorum* IV [Paris: Didot, 1851], p. 284 = Eusebius, *Praep. Ev.*, 457b).

19. Note, however, that in Creation tablet 4.39,40, Bel is preceded by light and his
body apparently is luminous. This is not affected by T.G. Pinches, 'A new Version of
the Creation-story', *JRAS* 23 (1891), pp. 393-408.

20. With reference to the separation of land and water, see n. 18 above. I think it
is plain that the work of Belus in this direction, which is immediately connected with the
building by Bel of the wall of Babylon, properly means the erection of the Semiramis-
mounds (Herodotus, 1.148) that prevented the flooding of the country. Berosus (in

Babylonian story is closely akin to the myths of savage nations, which make heaven and earth to be animated creatures originally locked together in a firm embrace, so that their children are crushed down in darkness. This, as Mr. Lang has well shown, is the original meaning of the Greek story of Kronos. The clearest form of the myth is that of New Zealand, where Tane Mahuta is the Demiurge who 'cruelly severed the sinews which united Heaven and Earth'.[21]

B. _Phoenician Cosmogonic and Primaeval Myths_

I pass now to the Phoenician myths and first to those which speak of the origin of heaven and earth. Here the best established point, which appears in three different versions,[22] is that the world came into being by the bursting in twain of a cosmic egg, such as also appears in Orphic speculation. The egg, says Mochus,[23] was broken in twain and one piece became heaven and the other earth. This egg takes the place of the Babylonian Tiamat. How the egg was burst is not so clear; but Mochus speaks of an opener whom he calls Chousoros. The name Chousoros has not been explained satisfactorily but he is evidently identical with the Chousor, who appears in another myth as a god, the inventor of iron and fishing tackle, and incantations and divinations, and as Zeus

Josephus, _Contra Apionem_, 142) says that the Greek writers are in error about the wonderful works they ascribe to Semiramis—that they will have confounded Bel's dyke with Semiramis's mounds (which were really tombs). I should like to know whether Išara is really = earth in general or = the _chōmata_ (mounds) near Babylon.

21. Lang, _Myth, Ritual, and Religion_, I, p. 302.

22. (a) In Philo (_Praep. Ev._ 33d), where we ought perhaps to read _Kai aneplasthē Mōt homoiōs ōiou schēmati_. At least the reference is to _Mōt_, not to the Zophasemin (= _ṣōpê šāmayim_). More probably _Kai aneplasthē_ etc. should precede _ēn de tina zōa...Hēlios kai selēnē_ is an explanation of _ouranou katoptai_. What is to be done with _kai exelampse Mōt_ I do not know. I think it comes later: _Kai exelampse Mōt, kai tou aeros diaugasantos_, i.e., _Mōt_ is egg-shaped—then heavenly bodies arise. Then Mot becomes full of light and the air is bright with the inflammation of land and sea. _Mōt_ may well be for _Tomōt = tᵉhōmôt_, as J. Halévy suggests (_Mélanges de critique et d'histoire relatifs aux peuples sémitiques_ [Paris: Maisonneuve, 1883], p. 387). But the _to_ will have been misunderstood and lost before Eusebius under Egyptian influence; (b) most clearly in Mochus at Damascius, 125c; (c) in Eudemus (also preserved in Damascius, 125c), where Lenormant has already silently corrected _ōton_ (owl!) to _ōion_ (egg); he should also have put _kaita = kai eita_ for _kata_.

23. See n. 22 (b).

Meilichios, that is as the king or Baal of some Phoenician town, apparently Sidon.[24]

Among the Phoenicians, as among the Chaldaeans, the world-egg is a watery mass which contains the germs of all life.[25] The heavenly bodies, according to one account in Philo, seem to have been formed in the womb of chaos, and the creation of male and female life in land and water is ascribed to the solar heat and the action of wind, cloud, rain and lightning which it sets up. Here we seem to have to do not with an original legend but with an attempt to philosophize the work of the Demiurge, who is identified with the sun, as Phoenician Baals often were in later times. The Phoenicians have something also to say about the origin of the world-egg. Here the accounts vary, introducing metaphysical conceptions like Time[26] and Desire.[27] These are probably modern additions, but all the accounts agree in a remarkable way in making the egg or *'ôlām*, the father of the egg, be preceded by the winds and by a murky turbid chaos, which is also called a mist (Omichle) or even Air. The primaeval world (*'ôlām*) seems to be conceived as condensed by the action of the winds on a thin dark misty chaos without limits. Here we have a view closely parallel to the brooding of the spirit of God on the face of the deep. In one account the world-egg is dropped altogether and the pair Aion and Protogonos, that is the 'primaeval world' (for the dualism is artificial throughout these theogonies), is the offspring of the wind Colpia (*rûaḥ kol pē'â*) and Baau

24. Chousor must have invented iron in order to cut open the egg. Cf. the arming of Bel in Creation tablet 4.30-62. Similarly, Kronos in the Byblian legend (Eusebius, *Praep. Ev.*, 36d) arms himself with sickle (*harpē*) and spear (*doru*) against Ouranos. Kronos too is aided by the incantations given by Hermes, who was with Athena, his counsellor, in preparing weapons. Is then Hermes = Chousor or is he a double and Kronos = Chousor? *Anoigeus* 'opener' in Damascius will be something from *ptḥ* 'open', presumably a rendering of Egyptian Ptah = Hephaestus. Cf. the Pataikoi in Herodotus, 3.37, who have the form of Ptah and are borne on ships, as Chousor was the first voyager. As Mochus is a Sidonian, Chousor is presumably a Sidonian god and (if I am right) = Eshmun or the brother of Eshmun if, as seems possible, the deeds of the two brothers have got jumbled. Note that Eshmun is a prophetic god. Agreus and Alieus the parents of Chousor are = Sidon.

25. Eusebius, *Praep. Ev.*, 33c.

26. Eudemus (n. 22), Chronos, Mochus, (n. 22) Oulomos = *'ôlām*, cf. *Aion*, Eusebius, *Praep. Ev.*, 34b,c.

27. Eusebius, *Praep. Ev.*, 33c; Eudemus (n. 22).

(*bōhû*).[28] Vegetation in this account appears in the primaeval world, and the next generation colonize Phoenicia and begin to worship the sun as Baal of Heaven. After these myths of the creation of heaven and earth and life generally we find a series of myths which are essentially theogonic. For these we have only Philo's authority and he makes all the gods mere deified men. Of the creation of man no separate myth has been preserved, and it is probable that most Phoenician races, certainly the kingly ones, claimed to be simply children of their local gods.

I do not propose to go at length through the theogonies, which are very confused and made up from a variety of local myths; but I will select some points that are characteristic or interesting.

First, I will observe that the Byblian theogony rests on an old creation myth like that of the Maoris or of Kronos in Greece, in which heaven and earth were represented as originally locked together in a close embrace and separated by their children, especially by the god El, who is the leader of his brethren in the matter. The details are similar to those of the well-known Greek myth in Hesiod and doubtless the story as we have it has been touched by Greek influence; though on the other hand the Greek story itself may have come in part from the East.[29]

---

28. Eusebius, *Praep. Ev.*, 34b.

29. The following particulars, however, are noticeable:

(1) Heaven (Ouranos) was not originally Heaven but was called Epigeios, or Autochthon (Eusebius, *Praep. Ev.*, 36b), i.e. he was not separated from his spouse the Earth.

(2) The arming of El with sickle and spear against his father is told particularly (Eusebius, *Praep. Ev.*, 36d). This is like the arriving of Bel in the Creation tablet and the invention of iron by Chousor, the opener of the world-egg. Is Chousor also *pattāḥ* and is this *Pataikos*, or rather was Ptah-Hephaestus, whom the Pataikoi resemble (Herodotus, 3.37), taken as *pattāḥ*? Again Kronos builds the walls of Byblos (Eusebius, *Praep. Ev.*, 37a), as Bel in *Praep. Ev*, 457b builds those of Babylon and as Chousor's brothers invent *toichous* 'house walls' (not indeed *teichē* 'city walls').

(3) The mutilation of Ouranos takes place 'in an inland place' (Eusebius, *Praep. Ev.*, 38b), unless indeed *mesogeiōi* here means 'subterannean' (against usage).

(4) The blood of Ouranos is transferred to fountains and waters 'and the place is still shown' (Eusebius, *Praep. Ev.*, 38b). Is there a parallel in the Babylonian legend in the transference of the blood of Tiamat by the North wind to hidden places? To the hidden South or to the North where the wind has his home? In the latter case it will be the source of Euphrates and Tigris. Cf. Job 26.7.

(5) As Ouranos was deified (*aphierōthē*) when he lost his private parts (*aidoia*) (Eusebius, *Praep. Ev.*, 38b), I do not doubt that it was by this part that he was attached to Ge. I suspect too that Ge is only a double of Berouth = *bᵉ'ērôt*, the mother of

A trait in the cosmogony which is very prominent and hardly due to the inventive Euhemerism of Philo is the connection of particular persons in the theogony with the invention of useful arts and with forms of religious observance. The same thing is seen to a limited extent in the oldest parts of the book of Genesis (J_1) and especially in the genealogy of the descendants of Cain. Here, for example, Cain (or Enoch) is the first city-builder, Jabal is the father of tent-dwellers, his brother Jubal of musicians and Tubal-Cain is the first smith (Gen. 4.17, 20-22). It is to be presumed that something of the same sort was found in the old Phoenician traditions that lay before Philo, though in these the inventors were doubtless gods or demigods, not men. Philo may have expanded and added to his sources, but he was not a pure inventor, at least as regards those figures in his genealogies that are real gods and of whom he himself says that they were worshipped after their death.

Let us look at the statements that come into direct comparison with the double story. Philo was of Byblos and therefore his first walled city is Byblos and the walls are the works of El or, as he is called in Greek, Kronos.[30] El is the creator of the Berytian legend as Bel-Marduk is in

Kronos, for in this Ge is both his mother and his wife. The b^e'$\bar{e}r\hat{o}t$ then are the inland place.

(6) There must be an explanation for the mutilation taking place in the 32nd year of the reign of Kronos (Eusebius, *Praep. Ev.*, 38a-b). Here clearly *two* legends are mixed and adjusted by a date. Now the era of Byblos begins with Kronos's accession, we must suppose. Does the other story come from a city with an era 32 years later? The era of Byblos, says B.V. Head, *Historia Numorum* (Oxford: Clarendon Press, 1887), p. 669, begins either 20 BC or 6 BC. Something older is probably meant. It may be noted that in Eusebius, *Canons*, Atlas is put in the year 378 or 380 after Abraham and *sūros gēgenēs*, the eponym of Syria, in the year 400 after Abraham (Migne, *Patrologiae cursus completus*, cols. 158-60). This would suit, since Atlas appears in the first story of Kronos. The Syrian legend, one supposes, may belong to Berothah (or Berothai) in Coele-Syria (Ezek. 47.16; 2 Sam. 8.8), or more likely Heliopolis itself, to which Constantine moved the Aphacans. Note, however, that Stephanus of Byzantium and Nonnos make Berytus a foundation of Kronos (which is also implied in Philo, when Kronos gives it to Poseidon) and gives a derivation from Ber = *phrear*, 'a well'. The Phoenician form, however, must have been plural, for Histiaeus says *bērouti = ischus*, from which Helladius takes the town's name (Müller [ed.], *Fragmenta historicorum Graecorum* IV, pp. 433-34). I think, therefore, that *Bērōth* and Beirut must be connected and, if so, one of the myths may be connected with the source of the Nahr Beirūt. If it is Beirut, *mesogeiōi* must be *under* the earth.

30. In *CIS* 1.1, a male deity of Gebal (Byblos) appears in personal names under

Babylon. Bel also builds the walls of Babylon—each city makes its own founder the Demiurge. In other legends, apparently belonging to other towns, we have things of the same kind. Thus at Tyre the founder Hypsuranios or *š^emê mārôm*, is the first to think of huts of reeds (?Adonis booths). Bricks and roofs and house-walls are put some generations later, perhaps by the inventive fancy of the Euhemerist, since the inventors bear very suspicious names and hardly can be real gods. The shepherd Jabal has perhaps his Phoenician parallel in Amynos and Magos, the inventors of villages and folds (or on another reading, flocks).[31] Jubal may be compared with Sidon, the woman with an incomparable voice who first discovered melodious hymns.

More important is the invention of iron and of this Phoenician legend has much to say. In the Byblian legend Chousor and his brother invent the working of iron and Chousor further devises hooks, baits and all the apparatus of fishing. In another legend iron is devised to enable the Demiurge to cut heaven and earth apart. As becomes a maritime people, all the local myths have something to say about the gods who first sailed the sea. In most early myths a prominent place is given to the invention of fire, and the absence of any legend of this kind from the Old Testament is one of the clearest proofs of the long interval that separates the book of Genesis from the ordinary traditions of early races. The Phoenician stories about this matter are curious and deserve some attention.

Philo first mentions the invention of fire in a context which his Euhemerism has carefully purged of mythical elements.[32] It was discovered, he says, by three mortal men called Light, Fire and Flame and was produced by rubbing two pieces of wood together. This is the old Arabian way of getting fire and indeed appears all over the world in early times and also in later times in connection with ritual. It is not

the titles *melek* and *'ādōn*, but the sovereign of the city is the *Ba'^alat G^ebal*, the *Baaltis hē kai Diōnē* of Eusebius, *Praep. Ev.*, 38d. For sovereigns of Byblos with names compounded of El, see Head, *Historia Numorum*, p. 668, including Enylos (Arrian, *Anabasis Alexandri*, 2.20.1). El here is presumably Adonis and, except in the cosmogonic myths, quite subordinate to Astarte.

31. Technites = in the parallel legend Amynos = *'āmôn* and Magos = Magar (*m^e'ārâ*)? Perhaps this is not pure invention, for the *koiranos kōmōn = Ba'al marqōd* = Megrin (accusative) in the inscription in C. Clermont-Ganneau, *Recueil d'archéologie orientale* I (Paris: E. Leroux, 1888), pp. 94-96, may be lord of Magaria villages.

32. Eusebius, *Praep. Ev.*, 34d.

improbable that it was some ritual usage that preserved the memory of
the primaeval firestick in Phoenicia.

But another fire myth appears a little farther on in a Tyrian legend.

> A violent tempest of wind and rain having arisen, the trees in Tyre were
> caused to rub on one another and caught fire, which burned down the
> wood there. But Usous, brother of Hypsuranios, the founder of Tyre,[33]
> took a tree and stripping it of its branches, was the first to venture upon the
> sea, and he consecrated two pillars to fire and wind and did them worship
> and poured out to them libations of the blood of the beasts he took in
> hunting.

For Usous, we are told, was a huntsman who invented the use of skins
as clothing. Eusebius's extracts from Philo are so mixed that it is not
quite safe to connect Usous's first beginnings of navigation with the fire,
and yet, when we read that he erected two pillars to fire and wind, it
must seem probable that it was the invention of fire that made a ship
possible. Iron had not yet been invented, that discovery is spoken of a
little later; so perhaps the myth was that the first ship was a canoe
hollowed out by burning such as savage peoples still use.

Be this as it may, the fire among the trees of Tyre appears in another
form in a legend preserved by Achilles Tatius and Nonnos and
commemorated on coins. In Tyre, says Achilles Tatius (2.14), 'the olive
and fire live together. A sacred spot enclosed in a wall sends forth an
olive tree with bright branches. A natural fire plays round the boughs
with much flame and its smoke (ash?) makes the tree thrive.' Nonnos[34]
tells the same story with the addition that the olive tree grew from two
rocks floating in the sea, that a dragon was coiled in the branches and
an eagle and a cup were poised on the summit. Under the direction of
Heracles the founders of Tyre sailed out from the mainland in the first
ship ever made and seized and sacrificed the eagle, whereupon the rocks
became fixed as two hills on which Tyre was built. One cannot lay
weight on details found in Nonnos alone, who uses all the freedom of an
epic poet. But coins of the Roman empire,[35] to which perhaps he was
indebted for his imagery, show the olive tree with its luminous branches

---

33. Hypsuranios = $š^e m\hat{e}$ $m\bar{a}r\hat{o}m$, the founder of Tyre is not the sun but the starry
sky = the Heracles Astrochiton, who is Archegetes of Tyre in Nonnos, *Dionysiaca*,
40.408. But is this conception old? Hardly.

34. Nonnos, *Dionysiaca*, 40.463-92.

35. Cf. coin of Gordian III, in Pietschmann, *Geschichte der Phönizier*, p. 295.

standing between the ambrosian stones,[36] that is the two pillars of Melqart, which Herodotus describes as of gold and Smaragdus[37] shining by night (2.44).[38]

The sacred olive tree of Nonnos, with the eagle and the serpent that guard it, reminds us of the tree of life guarded by griffins and other monsters, which appears not uncommonly on Phoenician and Assyrian designs. These monsters correspond to the Hebrew Cherubs, the guardians of the inner sanctuary and of the tree of life in the garden of Eden. In the latter case the flaming sword answers to the lambent flame round the Tyrian tree. It is not doubtful that the Cherubs of Solomon's temple were borrowed from Tyre and it is somewhat notable that they are called in 1 Kgs 6.23 *kᵉrûbîm ᵃ sê šemen* (which may perhaps be properly oleaster rather than the grafted olive). Olive trees are mentioned in Neh. 8.15. Note also the two olive trees in Zechariah 4, which stand beside the bowl (*gullâ*) on the top of the golden candlestick and feed its flame and are said to be 'the two sons of oil that stand before the Lord of the whole earth' (Zech. 4.14). The imagery here has a surprising resemblance to the furniture of the Tyrian sanctuary.

But there is another passage of the Old Testament, Ezekiel 28, where the allusions to the Tyrian sanctuary are unmistakable. In this chapter I think we must distinguish the prince (*nāgîd*) of Tyre in vv. 2-10 from the king of Tyre (*melek ṣôr*) in the elegy, vv. 12-19. In that elegy the prophet describes the fall of Melqart, the god 'full of wisdom and perfect in beauty'. The king of Tyre was 'in Eden, the garden of God'. His covering was of precious stones and his place was in the 'holy mountain of God', where he walked between the fiery stones. Now these fiery

36. There was a similar olive tree at Gades, not living but of gold (Philostratus, *The Life of Apollonius of Tyana*, 5.5). It is the olive of Pygmalion.

37. The Smaragdus fruit will represent a luminosity in the branches. As in Nonnos the sacrifice is offered to the rocks. These will be properly the pillars, not the island.

38. It would be easier to bring Philo and the other legend together if we can suppose that the sacred olive alone escaped conflagration or sprang up again like the olive tree at Athens after the burning of the Acropolis. Theophrastus, *Enquiry into Plants*, 2.3 and Pliny, *Natural History*, 17.241 probably refer to this. After all, why does Theophrastus use the vague expression he does if he means to refer to an Attic legend? William Ridgeway points out to me that Philo's burning of the forest has an exact parallel in Thucydides, *History*, 2.77, where he had long suspected a sacred legend to be referred to, and the language of Achilles Tatius would be best explained if there was a fire from which only the sacred olive arose fresher than ever. The olive of Pygmalion at Gades is an olive that springs up under the *pa'am* of the god.

stones are plainly the luminous pillars of Melqart and the holy mountain of God the rock on which the temple stood and where the whole is pictured as Eden, the garden of God, and the king as its Cherub.[39]

I think we may now go a step further and say that the scenery of Eden—the trees, the Cherubs, and all the other details, which must be treated allegorically if we are to give any spiritual meaning to the story—is in great part the scenery of the Phoenician sanctuary. The tree and the serpent, the Cherubs and the flaming sword are all to be found at Tyre, and from there the Hebrew story borrows its imagery, though it puts a new meaning into it.

I have now about exhausted my time; but I still must glance very briefly at one or two other points that show an affinity between Phoenician legend and the oldest narratives in Genesis. One of these points is the existence of a gigantic race which in Genesis are the off-spring of the sons of God and the daughters of men (Gen. 6.1-4). In Philo the giants are named from the Mountains of Syria, that is Lebanon, Antibanus, Mt Casius and Brathy.[40] They are, in fact, the Baalim of these mountains—cf. *1 En.* 6.6,[41] where Hermon is the seat of what is told in the Bible form of the story. From this one sees that the native Canaanite views influenced the Jews themselves in their interpretation of the biblical data. These giants are perhaps the *gēgeneis* of Nonnos,[42] who beget the race of Tyre by marrying the springs of the city.

Other points of contact are: (1) the sacrifice of an only son is told several times over; (2) the huntsman Usous, against whom his brother rebels; (3) the serpent is the wisest of animals, but in Phoenicia he has nothing to do with a fall; (4) the six-winged figure of Kronos may be compared with the seraphim.

To these various things might be added from other sources. For example, it is very probable that Justinus, *Epitoma historiarum Philippicarum Pompei Trogi*, 18.3, which speaks of the Phoenicians being driven from their first seats by earthquake and having dwelt by the [As]syrian lake before they settled on the Sidonian shore, may refer to the destruction of Sodom and Gomorrah. Or again, as Noah in the

---

39. We have also a possible allusion to the sacred olive tree, the Tyrian tree of life, in the word *mimšaḥ* (Ezek. 28.14).

40. Eusebius, *Praep. Ev.*, 34d.

41. Smith, *Religion of the Semites*, (1st series, 1st edn), p. 427 (= 2nd edn, p. 446).

42. Nonnos, *Dionysiaca*, 40.429-68.

Bible is the first to plant the vine, so the Tyrians had a legend of the god Dionysus first teaching a Phoenician shepherd the use of the grape.[43]

All this shows that Phoenician and Hebrew legends covered much the same general ground, but the similarity in material details only brings into more emphasis the entirely different spirit and meaning. The Phoenician legends are bound up throughout with a thoroughly heathen view of god, man and the world. Not merely are they destitute of ethical motives, but no one who believed them could rise to any spiritual conception of deity or any lofty conception of man's chief end. The Hebrew stories in Genesis, looked at in their plain sense, contain much that is not directly edifying. They do not make the patriarchs models of goodness, but they never make religion involve the approbation of a lower morality or a low view of the deity. In them God communes with men without ever lowering himself to the level of man. He had no human passions or affections, for his love to his chosen people was raised far above the weaknesses of human preferences. Above all, he was the God of the world before he was Israel's God, while in all the Semitic legends the Demiurge himself was always, and above all, the local king.

The burden of explaining this contrast does not lie with us: it falls on those who are compelled by a false philosophy of revelation to see in the Old Testament nothing more than the highest fruit of the general tendencies of Semitic religion. That is not the view that study commends to me. It is a view that is not commended but condemned by the many parallelisms in detail between Hebrew and heathen story and ritual. For all these material points of resemblance only make the contrast in spirit more remarkable.

43. See Achilles Tatius, 2.2.

Second Series, Lecture 1: Feasts

The Daily Free Press
Monday, March 3, 1890

The Religion of the Semites
Professor Robertson Smith on Semitic Institutions

Professor Robertson Smith, of Cambridge University, began the second course of Burnett Lectures on 'The Religious Institutions of the Ancient Semites' in the Hall of Marischal College on Saturday afternoon. There was a large attendance. Professor Robertson Smith said the short course of three lectures which it had been arranged he should deliver this spring would be concerned with some of the further developments of the religious institutions of the Semites. The fundamental principles, especially as regarded the fundamental act of ancient worship—sacrifice—were dealt with last year. There remained, however, a great multitude of derivative institutions, many of which were more important than even fundamental principles. In this short course he had been able only to select those points which seemed perhaps the most important and interesting in their bearing on the Old Testament religion. The lectures were less finished than they ought to be for such an audience. He had accumulated a large mass of notes upon the topics on which he intended to speak, but he was himself seized with a severe illness before he had made a selection of the points which would have been most suitable for the present lecture, and they were all aware that during the last few days other reasons had prevented him giving the attention that he ought to the subject. Professor Smith's subject was 'Festal Observances'. The character of ancient sacrifice, he said, made it necessarily a communal act, and those sacrifices were mainly performed at feasts—that was at occasions when a multitude of worshippers, representing as far as possible a whole community of one religion, were gathered together to do common service. It was customary to have sacrificial feasts in the spring season, and the choice of the season appeared to have been determined mainly in this manner that throughout Arabia all domestic animals as a rule had their yeilding [*sic*]¹ time in the spring. Professor Smith detailed the evidence that existed to show the relationship of the offering of the firstlings with the Passover. While all the spring fairs and spring feasts, he said, possessed many features in common, their time varied

---

* For a brief account of the discovery and obtaining of the press reports, see above, pp. 11-13.
1. Smith's original manuscript reads 'yeaning'.

considerably. Such exact dates as were ultimately obtained were not possible until such a stage of civilisation had been reached that the Kalendar was accurately fixed on astronomical principles. With all the ancient Semites the months were lunar. They averaged a length of $29\frac{1}{2}$ days. That gave a year of 354 days, or 10 less than it ought to be; so that in the course of about three years the months would be about 30 days different. In order to get the months and season of the year together, it was necessary to have recourse to a system of interpolation; and a complete system could only be obtained on astronomical principles. The closeness with which the spring feasts of the different Semitic nations fell together, and the closeness with which they agreed to the Passover were much too remarkable for it to be merely due to accident. They found that whether by biblical authority or not the pastoral feast of the Passover ultimately did come to be at the same time an agricultural feast. That was the tendency they found everywhere among the ancient religions. As soon as agriculture came to be the main means of living among the people it came to be felt—and rightly felt—that the good gifts of the field were those in connection with which men were specially called to appear before God—partly to offer Him their thanks, partly to offer Him tribute, and partly to ask His blessing on future crops and a continuance of fruitful seasons. The three good things that heathen nations wished of their gods were victory in war, multiplications of flocks and herds and the people's own progeny, and blessing upon the fruits of the earth. The causes which operated in agricultural nations to bring feasts, even when originally of a different origin, into connection with the season of harvests and vintage operated also in other directions in societies that were not agricultural. The lecturer having elaborated this point went on to say that there were remains of Kalendars in which the different feasts of different towns of the Semites have been all thrown together in such a way as to almost defy analysis. So far as one could see every city originally had its harvest feast, its vintage feast, and perhaps its spring pastoral feast, but of course in each city these feasts would be dedicated to the particular god of the city. Originally these feasts would be at the same time, or if they varied, they would only vary in so far as the seasons differed. In these later Kalendars they found such a medley of feasts working through each other in an unintelligible way that he could not attempt to analyse them. Some persons had sprung to the conclusion that all Semitic worship was originally worship of the heavenly bodies. Nothing could be more improbable. To make out in detail precise parallels was very difficult. They could make out a distinct parallel to Passover, but the Pentecost, the Feast of Harvest, and the Feast of Ingathering were not so easily brought into parallel with other Semitic observances. The next lecture will be given today.

The Aberdeen Journal

Monday, March 3, 1890
Professor Robertson Smith on Semitic Institutions

The second course of the Burnett Lectures on 'The Religious Institutions of the Ancient Semites' was commenced on Saturday afternoon by Professor Robertson Smith in the hall of Marischal College. The attendance was large. The lecture was occupied with a comparison of the annual feasts of the Hebrews as described in the

Old Testament and the analogous institutions subsisting amongst their heathen neighbours. The most interesting portion lay in an account of the spring feasts, of which traces remain connected with the story of the flood. At the outset Professor Smith said the short course of three lectures which it had been arranged he should deliver this spring would be concerned with some of the further developments of the religious institutions of the Semites. The fundamental principles, especially as regarded the fundamental act of ancient worship—sacrifice—were dealt with last year. There remained, however, a great multitude of derivative institutions, many of which were more interesting than even fundamental principles. In this short course he had been able only to select those points which seemed perhaps the most important and interesting in their bearing on the Old Testament religion. The lectures were less finished than they ought to be for such an audience. He had accumulated a large mass of notes upon the topics on which he intended to speak, but he was himself seized with a severe illness before he had made a selection of the points which would have been most suitable for the present lectures, and they were all aware that during the last few days other reasons had prevented him giving the attention that he ought to the subject. The subject of that day's lecture was 'Festal Observance'. The character of ancient sacrifices, he said, made it necessarily a Communal act, and those sacrifices were mainly performed at feasts when a multitude of worshippers, representing as far as possible a whole community of one religion, were gathered together to do common service. It was customary to have sacrificial feasts in the spring season, and the choice of the season appeared to have been determined mainly in this manner that throughout Arabia all domestic animals as a rule had their yealing [*sic*][2] time in spring. Professor Smith then detailed the evidence that existed to show the relationship of the offering of firstlings with the Passover, and subsequently pointed out how in this particular spring feast there was evidence of the way in which, through all the changes of religion, one and the same religious occasion could be carried on. While all the spring feasts possessed many features in common, their time varied considerably. Such exact dates as were ultimately obtained were not possible until such a stage of civilisation had been reached that the Kalendar was accurately fixed on astronomical principles. With all the ancient Semites the months were lunar. They averaged a length of $29\frac{1}{2}$ days. That gave a year of 354 days or 10 less than it ought to be: so that in the course of about three years the months would be about 30 days different. In order to get the months and season of the year together, it was necessary to have recourse to a system of interpolation, and a complete system could only be obtained on astronomical principles. The closeness with which the spring feasts of the different Semitic nations fell together, and the closeness with which they agreed to the Passover were much too remarkable to allow it to be supposed that it was a mere affair of accident. They found that whether by Biblical authority or not the pastoral feast of the Passover ultimately did come to be at the same time an agricultural feast. There was this tendency which they found everywhere among the ancient religions. As soon as agriculture came to be the main means of living among the people it came to be felt—and rightly felt—that the good gifts of the field were those in connection with which men were specially

2.   See n. 1.

called to appear before God—partly to offer Him their thanks, partly to offer him tribute, and partly to ask His blessing on future crops and a continuance of fruitful seasons. The three good things that heathen nations wished of their gods were victory in war, multiplication of flocks and herds and the people's own progeny, and blessing upon fruits of the earth. The causes which operated in agricultural nations to bring feasts, even when originally of a different origin, into connection with the season of harvests and vintage operated also in other directions in societies that were not agricultural. The lecturer having established this point went on to say that there were remains of kalendars in which the different feasts of different towns of the Semites have been all thrown together in such a way as to almost defy analysis. So far as one could see, every city originally had its harvest feast, its vintage feast, and perhaps its spring pastoral feast, but of course in each city these feasts would be dedicated to the particular god of the city. Originally these feasts would be at the same time, or if they varied, they would only vary in so far as the seasons differed. In these later kalendars they found such a medley of feasts working through each other in an unintelligible way that he could not attempt to analyse them. Some persons had sprung to the conclusion that all Semitic worship was originally worship of heavenly bodies. Nothing could be more improbable. It was very difficult to make out in detail precise parallels among other nations. They could make out a distinct parallel to Passover, but the Pentecost or Feast of the Harvest and the Feast of the Ingathering were not so clearly brought into parallel with other Semitic observances. The next lecture will be given today.

Second Series, Lecture 2: Priests and the Priestly Oracle

The Daily Free Press
Tuesday, March 4, 1890

The Burnett Lectures
Priests and the Priestly Oracles

Professor Robertson Smith delivered the second of the present course of Burnett Lectures on the Semitic Religious Institutions in the hall of Marischal College yesterday. The subject, he said, which he had announced for that lecture was that of 'Priests and the Priestly Oracle', and he proposed again to follow the method adopted in the last lecture of dealing mainly with those points in which it was possible to draw an interesting or instructive comparison between the priesthoods of the heathen Semites and the priesthoods of Israel. And he wished to begin by calling attention to the definition of the main function of the Old Testament priesthood under the law, which was given in the Epistle to the Hebrews. There, in the fifth chapter, in the revised version, they read that 'every high priest being taken from among men, is appointed for men in things pertaining to God, that he may offer both gifts and sacrifices for sins'. In another passage of this same Epistle a similar definition was extended, according to the true reading of the Greek text, 'and every priest standeth day by day ministering and offering oftentimes the same sacrifices, which can never take away sins.' That was not intended to be a complete account of the functions of the Old Testament priests, but it was a just statement of the main function which distinguished the Aaronic priesthood under the law from the time of Ezra to the final destruction of the Temple. The theory of the law was that the one true earthly sanctuary was of such terrible and consuming sanctity that the laity dared not come close to it to touch the holy things, and lay the gifts with their own hands upon the altar, but required the mediation of a consecrated priest, who, in virtue of his consecration and sanctity, was able to approach with impunity the holy things. Further, the gifts and sacrifices regularly presented by the priests were the necessary means towards the forgiveness of sins, and thus under the law the whole economy of Divine grace turned upon the mediatorial office of the priesthood. This conception of a mediatorial priesthood was not peculiar to the Old Testament, it appeared in several other of the more developed religions of the ancient world. Among the Brahmins and the Zoroastrians the assistance of the priests was necessary to the right performance of every religious act, and in ancient Babylon the influence of the priests was no less considerable, but the influence of the priesthood ultimately attained to as indispensable mediators between God and man was not primitive, but a thing of gradual growth. Savage nations, it was true, had something analogous to a priesthood in their sorcerers and medicine-men, and no doubt something of the sorcerer or medicine-man could still be traced in certain ancient priesthoods even in times of civilisation, but the view that the priest was a mere development of the sorcerer failed altogether in many of the higher religions, notably in the religion of Greece. In the Epistle to the Hebrews the priest was defined as the representative of the worshippers before God, especially in the sacrificial ritual connected with the forgiveness of sins, and the interest turned mainly on the exclusion of the worshippers from direct contact with the altar. This law of exclusion of the laity from immediate approach to the altar and other holy things could clearly be shown not to be ancient among the Hebrews. The ancient legislation of Genesis was addressed, not to the priests, but to the people at large, and, moreover, the provision, 'Thou shalt not go up the steps unto mine altar' was addressed, not to the priests, but to the people at large, and necessarily so addressed, for in later times, when only priests had permission, the altar had steps by which the priests ascended. Throughout the whole history of Israel they found constant examples of laymen approaching the altar and offering sacrifices. There were sacrifices of Gideon and Manoah, the repeated sacrifices of Saul, the sacrifices offered by David: there was the express statement that thrice a year Solomon himself drew nigh to the altar and offered sacrifice. Then there was the fact that some of David's sons were priests, and they had in the northern kingdom the practice of Jeroboam. It appeared, therefore, that throughout this period the priestly mediatorship, in the sense in which it was recognised by the later law, was not yet felt to be indispensable. In discharging the priestly function, the king might be said to discharge it in a representative sense, but there was a long step from this exercise of the priestly function and the institution of a separate priestly class. So long as the ceremonial was simple and tradition regulated the presentation of a sacrifice, it was natural that the civil heads of the community, the elders, or the king should represent the people in religious as they did in other ceremonies. This was the practice, they found, among the Arabs, and the same rule obtained in the most ancient societies. It was so in Greece and Rome, and he cited the parallel of king-priests in Greece and Rome mainly in order to show how unfounded was the Comtist doctrine about the priestly theocracies of the East. It was very common still to find people, whose knowledge of history was derived mainly from *a priori* sources, writing about a fundamental distinction between the constitution of the Eastern and Western Commonwealth, that, while the Western was essentially civil the eastern was essentially religious, and that the King was representative of the people, being supposed to be endowed with some special priestly sanctity. For this, so far as he could see, there was in history no foundation whatever. The ancient nations regarded the kingly power as sacred, but its sanctity was not derived from ritual or priestly privileges, nor enhanced by the performance of the sacred functions. Although the sacrificial functions of the priesthood might originally be exercised by any representative of the people, and especially by its natural representative, the civil head, the delegation of the sacrificial functions to a special priestly class arose very naturally as soon as society became very complex and the ritual very elaborate. And there were special reasons why in course of time the functions of the priesthood could be assigned to a separate class. Among these was [*sic*] the precautions in dress and otherwise that were necessary on approaching the altar, and which it was inconvenient for laymen to take, and there was also the difficulty of adequately mastering the details of the ritual. There were therefore abundant reasons for the gradual entrusting of the rite of sacrifice to a priestly class. Among the Semites, however, the priesthood originated in another direction, for the priests were in existence for another purpose before they began to be entrusted with this duty. In Arabia, priests were at first only found in places where there were temples and engaging in such parts of the ritual as were connected with the closed temple. The office was almost always hereditary in the family to which the sanctuary and the property of the holy place belonged—generally a great and noble family—so that the priests belonged for the most part to the leading families of Arabia. The priesthood ultimately attained to something of public importance as in the case of the hereditary custodianship of the Caaba, and in such a case it became a sort of freehold, to which were attached very considerable fees, derived from various sources. The office thus remained in the hands of a particular class, who, even in spite of the migrations of the tribes to which they belonged, retained the care of the temples as being supposed to be best acquainted with the gods of the land. The same practice recurred more or less exactly among other Semitic nations. There was the hereditary priesthood, for example, among the Phoenicians, and still closer was the parallelism found among the ancient Hebrews; closest of all was the parallel afforded by the very important history found in the Book of Judges of the sanctuary of the Ephraimite Micah. In that narrative by far the most important function of the early priesthood was that of consulting the oracle a function to which the sacrificial act was subordinate, although the two generally went hand in hand. Among the Arabs as among the Hebrews this consultation of the oracle was the reference of important disputes to the judgment of God Himself. It was in the discharge of this function that among the ancient Hebrews Moses procured decisions no man ventured to dispute, because they were the decisions of God and thus the law of God. The whole body of Hebrew law thus arose according to the usual method, from the accumulation of precedents. The Law of Moses was not a thing made in a moment, at one time, but the gradual growth of precedent, the decision of cases settled on appeal by the Divine oracle of the tabernacle. And the same thing happened long after in the case of Mohammed. The lecturer, then going back to an earlier stage of things, considered in detail the three chief methods of divine judgment in the sanctuary. First, and most important, the use of the sacred lot; second, the ordeal; and third, the oath of purgation.

The last of the present course of lectures will be delivered this afternoon at 4 o'clock.

The Aberdeen Journal
Tuesday, March 4, 1890

Semitic Priests and the Priestly Oracle

Yesterday afternoon Professor Robertson Smith delivered the second of the Burnett lectures on the religious institutions of the ancient Semites. The branch of this general subject he discussed was on 'Priests and the Priestly Oracle'. He devoted his remarks to showing that the supreme influence which the priesthood ultimately attained as the indispensable mediators between God and man was not primitive, but a thing of very gradual growth. In ancient times there was no such sharp line of demarcation between the laity and the priesthood as existed in Israel under the law, or such as was found in a community where the priests formed a separate hereditary caste. In those ancient times the sacrificer was the head of the community, who made the offering on behalf of the people, and in a sense the King might be said to discharge this representative duty, and therefore also the priestly function. This was the case with the chiefs in Arabia, in Greece, and in Rome. When the regal power ended the religious functions of the king were not distributed to the ordinary priests, who already existed, but were either distributed among the other civil officers of the Republic or transferred to a special officer who was the successor of the King for religious purposes only. He cited this mainly to show how unfounded was the ordinary doctrine about the priestly theocracy. Delegation of sacrificial functions to a special priestly class arose as soon as society became more complex and ritual more elaborate. It came to result, as a matter of convenience, that this sacrificial duty should be devolved on a special class. He instanced the illustrative case of worshippers making a circuit at Mecca, that forbade the worshippers devoting again to secular uses the clothing in which they made the circuit, and which clothing thus became holy. At Mecca, therefore, there arose those who hired clothing for the occasion, or else the worshippers who wished to be economical made the circuit naked. Exactly the same thing occurred in the worship of Baal. They would remember that the sacrificial dress showed that Jebu's soldiers [*sic*]³ were idolaters, and sentenced them to death. There was also knowledge of the details of ritual required, these details being necessary to the acceptableness of

---

3. 'Jebu's' is a misprint for 'Jehu's'. In fact, 2 Kgs 10.18-27 does not specifically mention Jehu's *soldiers* as idolaters.

the sacrifice. Clearly, therefore, there were abundant reasons for the gradual entrusting of the rite of sacrifice to a priestly class; but it did not appear that the priesthood among the Semites originated in that way. Rather its beginnings lay in another direction, and the priests already existed for other purposes before they began to be entrusted with altar duties. Here again he turned to the simplest of Semitic societies—Arabia. He said that many of the Arabic holy places consisted only of a sacred stone under the free heaven, but where there was a house or temple containing idols, or an oracle or the apparatus for an oracle, there was to be found a priest or keeper, who was custodian, not of the ritual of the sacred stone in front, but of such parts of the ritual as were connected with the inside of the temple. He explained that these complex accompaniments of the sacred stone could be provided, in such a poor country as Arabia, only by the wealthy or chief families, who appointed a member of their own family as custodian of this wealth in the form of ritual. But in other instances the custodianship of the temple, although it belonged to a particular family, was obviously an office of some importance to the State. The priesthood in such a case was a sort of valuable freehold. It no longer amounted to absolute property in the sanctuary, but was a freehold in regard to the very considerable position it afforded to the custodian of the temple from various sources. Of these, the first and most important was the oracle. Originally, the oracle was open to all members of the family, but when others came from a distance to consult it, then it became an office of profit. When tribes shifted from place to place the priest's inducement to remain was so great as to lead him often to break the ties even of kindred, and the new-comers who took the place of the tribe that had left were not disposed, for the most part, to dispossess the old priests, for good reasons. When the Assyrians who depeopled Samaria, were attacked by lions, which was in consequence of the increase of wild beasts after the depopulation, the incomers thought it was because their priests did not know the way of the gods of the land, and requested Hebrew priests to be sent to them. Professor Smith related the story of Micah, who hired a wandering Levite to take charge of the worship in his temple, as showing that at that time there was some beginning of the priesthood of the Levites. This was the second stage, where instead of a member of the family there was chosen for the priesthood a man supposed to possess a peculiar skill. And thirdly, the Danites carried off Micah's sacred things, and retained the service of the priest for them. This Levitical priest, the grandson of Moses, became the ancestor of Levitical priests who served the sanctuary of Dan down to the time of the captivity. Professor Smith next sketched the history of Arab society, which was akin to that of the Hebrews while they were wandering in the wilderness, to prove that the only judgment they would acknowledge was that of God. No Arab recognised any other Arab as his master, and hence the only judgment that was left to which they would submit was that of God. Thus Moses administered the judgment of God, and Mahomet became the Prophet or mouthpiece of God. Describing the methods of the divine element in the sanctuary, Professor Smith said these methods were three—(1) the use of the sacred lot, which was the most important; (2) the ordeal, as found among early nations; and (3) the oath of abrogation. He described these, devoting particular attention to the sacred lot, which he illustrated by a reference to Sennacherib [*sic*][4] whirling the arrows when he came to the parting of the ways in his advance against Jerusalem. He remarked that in Hebrew history the priestly lot was at first the most important way of obtaining a divine decision, but at a later time it fell in the background, and the prophetic lot took the first place as an oracle of revelation. Professor Smith intimated that the third and last lecture of the course would be upon 'Prophets and Divination'.

Second Series, Lecture 3: Priests (Contd), Diviners, Prophets

The Daily Free Press
Wednesday, March 5, 1890

The Burnett Lectures
Unique Character of the Hebrew Prophets

Professor Robertson Smith delivered the last of the present course of Burnett Lectures on 'Semitic Religious Institutions' yesterday in the hall of Marischal College. In the previous lecture, he said, they found that, while other methods of revelation were recognised and practised in connection with the worship of Jehovah, the consultation of the priestly oracle in ancient times held the first place amongst the means of revelation. That function, however, gradually declined in importance after the growth of prophecy, especially from the times of Elijah and Elisha. At the time of the great prophets, of whom they had written remains, the prophetic word took indisputably the first place amongst the means of revelation, for the work of the priests was now mainly confined, not to giving new decisions and consulting the priestly oracle, but to the maintenance of ritual tradition and other traditions of common law. After this the function of the priests as interpreters of sacred tradition and precedent declined in importance, because the law had been put in writing and circulated freely amongst the people, in fact its very interpretation fell very much out of the hands of the priests and into the hands of the scribes or learned classes. But what the priests lost in importance this way was compensated for by the prominence now attached to the mediatorial function in worship. From the time of the kingdom onwards, they found the splendour and magnificence of the temple service constantly increasing, the priesthood became more complicated, and a certain complexity of ritual was introduced that was quite foreign to the old shrines like that of Shiloh. Having briefly sketched the way in which the priesthood ultimately acquired something of a hierocratic character, the lecturer asked to be allowed to make a slight digression in regard to this matter. They were very well aware, he thought, of the large part that hierocratical ideas had played at certain periods in Christianity, and they knew that the hierarchy of the clergy had often been alleged to be based upon divine institution and derived from the priesthood of the Old Testament. These ideas, of course, prevailed

---

4.   This is an error—according to Ezek. 21.21 the king concerned is Nebuchadrezzar. Curiously, this appears to be Smith's own error, since in the manuscript of this lecture Smith wrongly refers here to the Assyrians (though Sennacherib is not mentioned by name).

entirely among the Roman Catholic Church, but something of the same sort was not wanting among other Episcopal Churches—(applause). It was, however, perfectly plain from history that the hierarchical power of the priests had absolutely no religious foundation whatever. It sprang up among the Semitic nations merely by political incidence, for the hierarchical power of the priests would never have been developed in a free nation, the development was only possible in nations in a condition of civil servitude—(applause). Passing on to consider the other methods of revelation practised among the Semites, he said that among the Hebrews, as among the other nations, the sacred lot was not the only recognised means of revelation. The means of consulting the Divine will were numerous, and our knowledge of them was pretty full, for in the warnings addressed to the Israelites, who were so prone to have recourse to methods of divination, a tolerably full catalogue was supplied of the different methods employed. There was in particular a very full account in the 18th Chapter of Deuteronomy. In that description some of the means of divination were condemned as being in their own nature heathenish, others were condemned only when conducted in a heathenish way in the name of other gods than Jehovah. The proper methods were found summed up under the general name of prophesy [*sic*]. There were prophets of Baal as well as prophets of the Lord, but to consult the prophets of Baal was wrong, on the ground that they did not prophesy in the name of Jehovah. And the same observation applied to the method of divination by dreams and visions. These were the arts only forbidden *secundum quid*. On the other hand there were certain arts absolutely forbidden, because in their own nature they were purely and necessarily heathenish. Thus the forbidden arts might be divided under the two heads of, first, divination pure and simple, and second, black art, meaning divination, with the magical element, involving the use of charms, material means to constrain the supernatural powers. The functions of pure divination presented a great similarity to the legitimate oracle or to the functions of the seer. In early Israel, they were illegitimate only when practised in the name of other gods. The magical arts, on the other hand, were put down as absolutely inconsistent with Jehovah worship. These he then proceeded to discuss in detail, treating of the use of incantations, serpent charming, the use of amulets, and the consultation of familiar spirits or ghosts. As to the latter they had a vivid description in the visit of Saul to the Witch of Endor. It did not appear in that story that Saul or those by whom he was accompanied saw a ghost, and, indeed, in general those who professed to have communication with spirits did not profess to show the spirits. It was rather made to appear as if the sound of the voice was made to issue from the ground or from the belly of the sorcerer, and in this way the latter sought to convey to [*sic*] idea to his dupes that the spirit entered into him and spoke out of him, and for this purpose he practised a sort of ventriloquism. The methods of pure divination mentioned in the Old Testament might be divided under the three heads—first, under a general term that included all forms of revelation, but primarily meant the consultation of the sacred oracle; next came that class of seers who gave oracles, not by signs, but by an inspired recitation—a class that was very common among the Semites of Arabia, but in regard to which it was peculiar that the Arabic seer always spoke in a kind of frenzy, the clearest mark of distinction between him and the true prophet who spoke sanely; thirdly, there was the form of divination by augury. Divination by augury was absolutely forbidden in the Old Testament, and if one considered the enormous slavery that attendance upon augury involved, the enormous paralysism of industry, one could judge that the emancipation from the slavery of such signs was one of the greatest practical boons conferred upon Israel by its religion—for the benefits of the religion were not limited to purely spiritual things, but were also in a very large degree a practical boon for the ordinary concerns of daily life, and in no respect more so than in this which he had just mentioned—(applause). Proceeding, he said they were now able to approach and criticise a statement often made nowadays that prophecy of the kind found in the Old Testament was not a thing peculiar to Israel but was a natural product of the Semitic race, characteristic of the Semitic nations as a whole. The way it was put was generally this, that the great founders of the Aryan race were philosophers, and those of the Semitic race were prophets. Those who took that view were thinking mainly of the Hebrews and the Arabs, thinking, among the Hebrews, of Isaiah, Jeremiah, Amos, and the other great teachers, and, among the Arabs, thinking chiefly of Mahomet, but also of other leaders of the race down to the present day. Only the other day, in a review of his first volume of these lectures, the writer, who from his observations, might be expected to know something of the subject, said he (Professor Smith) made a mistake in supposing that the Old Testament could only have been produced by the Hebrews, and could not have been produced in any other Semitic nation. In point of fact there was not the slightest historical evidence that anything the least like Amos, Isaiah, and Jeremiah was produced by any other Semitic nation, there was no evidence that any branch of Semites outside Israel ever rose to a religious condition in which such productions could have been possible. If they accepted the definition that made prophecy simply identical with prediction, then there was prophecy among the other Semites, but the Old Testament never allowed prophecy to be treated as merely the same thing as prediction, it did not rest the argument upon that. It certainly held that the prophets of Israel made true predictions, but it did not hold that that of itself alone was enough to make them true prophets. What constituted true prophecy was prediction combined with the evidence of the moral government of the world by the great King of Israel to which the prophets appealed—(applause). Those who held the view that the books of the Old Testament could have been produced by other Semites rested their argument mainly upon the prophet Mohammed, but on close examination it would be seen that the argument from Mohammed failed entirely. In the first place, Mohammed had nothing new to say, the whole substance of his utterances was the things he had learned from the Jews and Christians. It was indeed no exaggeration to say that there was not a single new religious idea, whether true or false, from beginning to end in Mohammed's revelation. There was certainly an amount of religious mythology, but that was not religious revelation, true or false it was not that. Then there was the peculiarity of the epileptic state not found in the Hebrew prophets, and, further, Mohammed's revelation was a book revelation—Christianity, he knew, was sometimes spoken of as a book revelation, but they would not find that in the Bible. There was no doubt in the Koran a great deal that was very remarkable and very original, but it was not religious. When Mohammed came to Medina and became the head of the community, and saw that he would be entrusted with the solution of political and social questions, he developed very great political ability, and to keep up his reputation he put his selfish policy into the form of revelation; but that, of course, was not true revelation, but merely the affectation of a religious guise employed by one of the most skilful politicians that ever founded an empire—(applause). The other leaders of the race who claimed to be prophets had been shown also to be deliberate impostors. Old Testament prophecy remained before as after historical investigation—a thing unique to the history of the world—(loud applause).

The Aberdeen Journal
Wednesday, March 5, 1890

Semitic Prophets and Divination

Yesterday afternoon Professor Robertson Smith delivered at Marischal College the third and concluding Burnett lecture on the religious institutions of the ancient Semites. His remarks on this occasion were confined to 'Prophets and Divination'. He said that after the exile the function of the priests as interpreters of sacred traditions and precedent declined in importance, because the law had been put in writing and circulated among the people—in fact, its interpretation passed from the priests into the hands of the Scribes or learned classes. The priests were compensated by the prominence attached to their mediatorial function in worship—in the growth in magnificence and complexity of the temple service. The magnificence was largely influenced by and copied from Canaanite and heathen practice. Solomon had his temple erected by Tyrian workmen, and from Tyrian designs. In like manner, in the elaborate organisation of priestly ceremonies, Caanan and Phoenicia seemed to have been taken as first models, care being exercised, of course, to exclude any feature that was inconsistent with Jehovah worship. Most of the kings, however, were by no means scrupulous even in this respect. Among things thus copied were the dress of the priests—the heathen priests being dressed exactly like the priests of Israel—the priests appearing to have ministered barefooted, and the regulations relating to sacrifice. Describing the usages in worship of the heathen Semites, he said they had devotees—not strictly priests—male and female, consisting of half-insane women and men who, if not insane, were required, in the interests of religion, to work themselves into a frenzy which the ignorant worshippers assumed to be divine worship, and at some of the shrines there were dancing women of the vilest character. While these practices were forbidden in Israel, they were frequently introduced. Concerning the dancing in Phoenician sanctuaries, for example, in the Bible itself, there was the curious account of the leaping and halting of the priests of Baal in the sacrifice at Mount Carmel. The halting was no doubt meant as something of a courtesy. This was the heathen origin of dancing dervishes in Mahomedan countries to this day. As regards the rationale of this dancing, he apprehended that in the first instance it was simply the natural expression of mirth, which frequently accompanied singing. Afterwards it became more and more an artificial ceremony, and care was taken to make it so frantic, by spinning round, as to confuse the head, and by other extra-ordinary superexcitations of the nervous system to induce a frenzy which the people ascribed to a supernatural cause. In Israel artificial frenzy of that sort was prohibited, but that there were tendencies to it was plain, for there was something of a frenzy in Saul when he came among the prophets. But the tendency of Jewish religion was all along against this materialistic frenzy. The characteristic of Hebrew prophecy was that it was sane and self-possessed. (Applause.) He gave particulars to show that it was through the influence their priestly functions brought them that the priesthood ultimately acquired something of a hierocratic character. It was the priestly house of the Maccabees, for instance, that led the tribes to victory, and in one person combined the function of the people's priest and prince. He mentioned this because his audience were well aware of the large part which hierarchical ideas had played in certain parts of Christianity. The hierarchy of the clergy had often been represented as based on divine institution and derived from the priesthood of the Old Testament. That idea prevailed entirely among the Roman Catholic Church, and something of the same sort was not wanting in many other Episcopal Churches. It was perfectly plain from history that the hierarchical power of the priests had absolutely no foundation whatever. (Applause.) Passing on to speak briefly of other methods of revelation practised among the Hebrews, he directed attention to various practices that were forbidden in the 18th chapter of Deuteronomy, and said that while certain heathen practices were absolutely forbidden to the Hebrews there were others that were analogous to those of the heathen, and that were forbidden only when conducted in the name of other gods than Jehovah. Of this latter kind were dreams and visions, though at the same time dreams and visions were appealed to comparatively rarely, except in the older part of the Bible narrative. Certain arts absolutely forbidden to the Hebrews were divination, pure and simple, and the black art—namely, magic or divination, with the magical element involved—which even Saul, though he might not be considered orthodox, put down as absolutely inconsistent with Jehovah worship. Of this nature were wizards who charmed by magical practices or incantations, the commonest kind of incantation among the Hebrews seeming to have been serpent charming, which was practised in some countries as a trick to this day. There were, no doubt, also among the lower classes of Hebrews charms for good or ill, such as were found in Scotland at a recent date, if they did not exist in some parts still. Speaking of forbidden amulet charms, such as Isaiah rebuked the daughters of Jerusalem for wearing, he said that among the Arab and Midianite races they were found of the shape of little moons, and were also described as like a horse shoe, and that last hint enabled them to identify the origin of putting a horse shoe over stable doors. (Applause.) He then commented on divination by ghosts, such as that of the witch of Endor, and to [*sic*] the producing by sorcerers of secret voices through ventriloquism and otherwise. Passing on to speak, under the head of pure divination, of a class of diviners who claimed to have an inspired recitation, and who spoke, under strong mental excitement, a language generally unintelligible and frequently having special interpreters, he said the peculiarity between the Arabic seer of this kind and the Hebrew seer was that the Arabic seer always spoke in a kind of frenzy, and so also did the seers of Greece. That was the clearest mark of distinction between them and the Hebrew prophet, who spoke sanely and with self-possession. As Paul put it, 'The spirits of the prophets are subject to the prophets.' Another form of pure divination was augury, which was strictly and absolutely forbidden in the Old Testament. If one considered the enormous slavery which the attendance on auguries involved, and the paralysis of industry resulting therefrom, they could judge that the emancipation from that slavery was one of the greatest practical boons conferred upon Israel by its religion. (Applause.) The assertion was often made nowadays that prophecy of the kind found in the Old Testament was not at all peculiar to Israel, but was a natural product of the Semitic race—characteristic of the Semitic nations as a whole. The other day he had read a criticism of his own lectures by a man who had showed by the nature of his criticism that he had a good knowledge of what he was writing on, but who had made the mistaken assertion above referred to. In point of fact there was not the slightest historical evidence that anything in the least like the books of Amos, Isaiah, or Jeremiah was produced by any of the heathen Semites—no evidence even that any branch of the Semites outside of Israel ever rose to the religious condition in which such prophecy would have been possible. (Applause.) There was plenty of mere chance prediction coming true in Semitic races other than Israel; but in no other nation was there prediction of the kind that foretold the captivity and the return from it, and the means by which these great events were brought about. It was not mere prediction itself, but prediction with the evidence of the moral government of the world by the King of Israel, to which the prophets of Israel appealed. He held it proved also that the Hebrew prophet was not a mere mechanical mouthpiece, but one who understood and sympathised with the purposes of the Lord while uttering the prophecy. He passed on to show that the prophecy of Mahomet was in the first place frenzied utterance of information he had gathered in his journeys as a camel driver, and that what he wrote later was dictated by the cold, calculating policy of one of the greatest politicians who ever founded an empire. Though the Koran was a remarkably clever book, it contained none of the marks of Divine origin that were to be found in the Bible. Old Testament prophecy remained, before as after investigation, a thing unique in the world's history. (Applause.)

Third Series, Lecture 1: Semitic Polytheism (1)

The Daily Free Press
Friday, December 11, 1891

The Burnett Lectures
Professor Smith on Semitic Religion

Professor Robertson Smith began the concluding course of three lectures in connection with his series of Burnett Lectures on Semitic religion in Marischal College yesterday. There was a large attendance. Principal Geddes presided, and among the audience were Sir John Clark of Tillypronie and Mr David Littlejohn, Sheriff Clerk, two of the Burnett Trustees.

Professor Smith, at the outset, said the subject that had been announced for this concluding course of lectures in Semitic religion was Mythology and Cosmogony. He was afraid that was not entirely descriptive, but he chose the word mythology rather than polytheism. The first two lectures would contain some mythological matter and a good deal of matter which hangs on that; he proposed in them to look at the main features of Semitic polytheism; the third lecture would be devoted to a consideration of the Semitic views as to the creation and government of the world. In beginning to talk of the characteristics of the Semitic polytheism, he should like to ask them a question—Did they remember the time when, as children, they first became acquainted with the Old Testament history? And did they remember being puzzled by what he well remembered was the great puzzle of that history to him—why were the Israelites so ready to go aside and worship other gods? What was there to attract them in the gods of their neighbours? He reminded them of this difficulty now, not that he might answer the question—at least, not at present—but because the very existence of such a difficulty was instructive as showing how entirely remote our modern habits of thought were from those in which the polytheism of the ancient Semites had its root. We all had our doubts and temptations in matters of faith, but we could not imagine ourselves tempted to believe in the Baalim and the Ashtaroth, whose worship had so fatal an attraction for the ancient people of Jehovah. This entire want of sympathy with the standpoint of Semitic heathenism was a grave obstacle to the scientific study of the subject. What we know of the Semitic gods, and of the beliefs of their worshippers concerning them, was all fragmentary, and to piece all those fragments together and build up from them a consistent account of Semitic polytheism as a whole, it was above all things necessary that we should be able to put ourselves alongside of the way of thinking to which those strange deities were conceivable, credible, and worthy of worship. If we carried our own modern habits of religious thought into the study, we should be liable at every moment to put a false construction on the facts before us, and draw inferences that the old heathen worshippers did not and could not draw. A great deal of what had been written about Semitic heathenism was vitiated by the neglect of this caution, and especially by the importation of modern metaphysical ideas where such ideas had no place. Almost everything written by Germans was dominated from first to last by theological conceptions of what the religion must have been rather than to [*sic*] any knowledge of what it was. But it was not enough to be chary in the use of modern ideas and categories. Much of our knowledge about the gods of the Semites comes to us from classical writers who saw the facts through a halo of Greek metaphysics, or at all events were apt to read them in the light of their own religious beliefs, and the consequence of this for the modern study of Semitic religions had been that too many Greek ideas had been introduced into what had been written on the subject. He imagined, therefore, that it would not be amiss and might serve to clear away misconceptions if he began what he had to say about the gods of the Semites by indicating some of the main points of contrast between them and the Hellenic deities. The great gods of Greece were sharply discriminated from one another in character, attributes, and functions. They formed an orderly community under the headship of Zeus, and each member of this community had a recognised sphere of divine activity corresponding to his special tasks and powers. It was true that the parcelling out of the governments of the world among the different gods and goddesses was not carried out with strict logical precision upon a single principle, and that conflicts of authority sometimes occurred in Olympus. But on the whole Zeus maintained tolerable order in his divine family. The main cause of discord among the gods was their interest in particular families and communities of men, which led them to take a share in the feuds of humanity. And this again meant mainly that Greek religion never entirely shook off the conception that the gods had a natural connection with certain races or certain localities. But Greek polytheism attained a substantial measure of system and unity by subordinating the local relations of the gods to the conception of special divine functions which each deity exercised, not on behalf of one family or city, but on behalf of worshippers without regard to their descent or birthplace. Accordingly, Greek deities were habitually thought of, not as the gods of particular tribes and towns, but as the patrons of certain arts and industries; the powers presiding over certain departments of nature and human life. The theory that each god had his own department gave an air of reasonableness to polytheistic worship. The Greek did not confine his service to a single patron, but addressed himself by turns to all the gods because each could do for his worshipper something that lay outside the province of the other deities. Again, the departmental theory gave to Greek religion a certain character of universality. All the divine powers that presided over nature and human life were represented in the Hellenic pantheon, and within his own sphere each god had a world-wide sway. From all this they might fix on three points as characteristic of Greek polytheism in its highest development. First—Although the gods had certain local connections and special predilections for particular places and people, their power was not limited to one place or their sovereignty to one community of men. Second—Every Greek had access to all the gods, and though, in virtue of his descent or his place of residence, he might look on one deity as his special patron, it was proper for him to recognise each god in turn, according to the nature of his varying needs. Third—The main reason for this was that each god had a special function connected with some particular department of nature or of human life. Let them now compare the state of the case as regarded the gods of the Semites. And first as regarded the extent to which gods were freed from connection with particular localities. There was clear evidence, as was shown in the first course of these lectures, that the oldest Semitic gods were tribal or local. As a rule, they were both tribal and local, for the local Baal, who had his home in a particular holy place, was also the ancestral god of the community that lived around his sanctuary. In this there was probably no fundamental antithesis to the Greek view, for most of the Greek gods had special predilections for particular sanctuaries, and it was highly probable that many of them, though they afterwards assumed a larger character, were originally nothing more than local or tribal deities. But in the case of the Greek gods this was more or less matter of speculation, and probably a majority of inquirers still held that the greater gods of Hellas were worshipped as cosmical powers by the undivided Aryans long before they found local seats in Hellas. No such position could be obtained with any degree of plausibility as regarded the Semitic gods, for here it was very clear that the local connection of the god involved a local limit to his power. In Semitic heathenism, and especially in the Baal worship of the Northern Semites, they could see that the connection of the gods with particular places was of a physical kind. The energy of the god had its centre at the sanctuary, where a holy fountain, or stream, or grove was revered as instinct with divine life; it was here that the worshippers appeared before their god with gesture of adoration and gifts of homage, and all the blessings which he conferred appeared in some sort to emanate from this centre. At a distance from the sanctuary the god was less powerful, and his habitual energy did not extend beyond his own land. A man who left his own people and settled abroad left his god behind him, and was compelled to become the client of a new religious worship. What he had described was the primitive type of local Baal-worship as it is found among the agricultural populations of Canaan and Syria in the oldest times of which there was any record. The physical conditions of Syria, where small regions of great fertility were separated by barren tracts and rough mountains, favoured the existence of small isolated communities, where alone this primitive type could be maintained unmodified. It was in these remote and isolated spots that they must look for the oldest type of Syrian religion, and sound method demanded that they should examine this type fully and learn all they could from it before they could attempt to deal with the more complex religious phenomena exhibited in the cults of great empires like Assyria, or great merchant cities like those of Phoenicia, which lay on the highways of international movement. Proceeding then to inquire whether they could realise more precisely how the power and activity of the god was conceived as radiating outwards from his sanctuary, the lecturer remarked that in some cases the conception appeared to have been almost purely physical—and here he sketched an example of a community of worshippers occupying the basin of a single stream, with practically one myth. That was the narrowest and simplest form of the physical conception. But the anthropomorphic conception of the god as king gave room for wider conceptions. Wherever the people went to extend their borders by occupying waste lands or encroaching on the territories of their neighbours, the god went with them, and the mere fact that they were able to establish themselves on new ground was sufficient evidence that they were still within the region over which their god had effective sway. He thought they could see that when the same god came to be worshipped simultaneously at many sanctuaries, and was held to be present at them all, a distinct step was taken towards a larger conception of the divine nature than that which was involved in the worship of the Baal of a single sanctuary. And from our point of view we might be apt to think that a god who could be present in many places at once was on a fair way to become omnipresent and shake off all local limitations, but it had to be remembered that in the ordinary service of a local sanctuary there was little or nothing to impress upon the worshippers that idea that the god whom they adored at their local altar was the god of the whole land. They would regard him especially as their local god dwelling in their midst, who might be reckoned on to take their part, not only against the enemies of the nation, but likewise in purely local matters, as in feuds with the people of a neighbouring town. In ordinary times this point of view would vastly outweigh the larger conception of Jehovah as the national god, for it was very evident from what was known of Semitic history that communal feeling was ordinarily far stronger than national feeling. This indeed was the chief reason why Semites had not played a larger part in the history of the world. They had several times had the opportunity of doing so, and had always been wrecked upon the communal feeling—what he supposed must be called Home Rule, the desire of each little group to manage its own affairs, and the desire not to subordinate its individual interests to the interests of the nation as a whole—(applause). Passing on, the lecturer proceeded to show how the idea that each god had a physical connection with one sanctuary and its district naturally produced the conception that however widely his influence might extend, and however his sanctuaries might be multiplied, the true centre of his divine energy, and the place where he was nearest to the prayers of his worshippers, was still his old primeval seat; and how this bore on the practice of pilgrimage. He pointed out that the grand distinction between Judaism and the other faiths of the Roman Empire was the fact that the Jews knew no holy place except Jerusalem, and that, though on one side the religion of Israel was finally cut off from the old materialistic basis of heathenism by the abolition of the local high places, it still kept touch with the lower Semitic faiths in retaining the temple of Jerusalem as a visible centre of Jehovah's sovereignty. In the closing part of the lecture, Professor Smith touched briefly on the worship of the heavenly bodies, and on the use of portable idols as an element of interest in connection with the local limitations of deity.

The next lecture will be given to-morrow afternoon at three.

The Aberdeen Journal
Friday, December 11, 1891

The Burnett Lectures—Concluding Series

Yesterday afternoon Professor W. Robertson Smith, LL.D., of Cambridge, delivered the first of his concluding series of Burnett Lectures in the hall of Marischal College, on 'The Religious Institutions of the Ancient Semites.' There was a large attendance. Professor Smith framed what he said about the gods of the Semites mainly on the lines of an indication of the chief points of contrast between them and the Hellenic deities. The oldest or Semitic gods were tribal or local. On the other hand, most of the Greek gods had special predilections for particular sanctuaries, but it was highly probable that many of them were originally nothing more than local or tribal deities. It must be remembered that the forms of worship at all sanctuaries were of a type that directly suggested a physical connection between the god and the holy place where he dwelt—in a sacred fountain or tree or pillar. This was a palpable notion easily grasped by everyone, while the notion that the same god had his seat at distant holy places was hard to grasp and lay outside the region of daily experience. Going on to speak of the distinction between Judaism and the other faiths of the Roman empire, he said the distinction lay in the fact that whereas the Jews knew no holy place except Jerusalem, the Tyrians set up altars wherever they went. Though on one side the religion of Israel was finally cut off from the old materialistic basis of heathenism by the abolition of the local high places, it still kept touch with the lower Semitic faith in retaining the Temple of Jerusalem as the visible centre of Jehovah's sovereignty.

Third Series, Lecture 2: Semitic Polytheism (2)

The Daily Free Press
Monday, December 14, 1891

The Burnett Lectures
Professor Smith on Semitic Religion

Professor Robertson Smith delivered his second lecture on Semitic religion in the Hall of the Marischal College on Saturday afternoon. There was a fairly large attendance.

Professor Smith said that in his introductory lecture he had spoken of the use of idols, and of the common use of small idols by private persons called away to a distance from the sanctuary, in order to secure the certain presence of the godhead. Continuing, he said that this ancient Hebrew custom practically prevailed in Arabia. These household images were rather amulets on a larger scale than gods in the full sense of the word. In great public expeditions of a protracted kind something more than this was needed; the national god must go forth with his people, and be accessible during the campaign in acts of public worship, or when an oracle was required for the conduct of the business in hand. This requisite was met by the institution of portable sanctuaries, which were to heathenism what the ark and the tabernacle were to the people of Israel. The invention of portable sanctuaries, and especially of portable idols, might possibly go back to the nomadic Semites, and to a time when the gods were still tribal rather than local; but the possibilities were against such a view. It was more likely that portable symbols of the godhead first arose among the settled Semites, and in connection with the religion of the army in war. The next point dealt with was the contrast between Semitic religion and the religion of the Greeks. The Greek had access to all the Hellenic gods, and he worshipped them all as fit occasion arose. There was no Pan-Semitic feeling like the Pan-Hellenic feeling that united the Greeks of different States in a common religious life in spite of their political feuds. When two Semitic States were at war their gods were at war also, and when one State crushed another it ravished its sanctuaries and destroyed its idols, or carried them off in captivity, not to be worshipped, but to stand as trophies in the temples of their captors. This was the standing practice of the Assyrians, and in like manner the Philistines carried off the ark to set it up in the Temple of Dagon. The heathen Semites did not deny that the gods of other nations were real gods, and powerful on their proper ground; but they had no occasion to worship them, for their native gods were sufficient, and they had no reason to think that their homage would reach the ear of gods that dwelt far off; or, if it did reach them, that it would find acceptance with the hereditary duties of foreigners and enemies. There was a broad distinction between this point of view and that of the Greeks, with whom the conviction that the same gods ruled in all lands was so strong that they detected Greek deities under foreign names whenever they visited a strange country. The Semitic principle that no man had anything to do with the gods that were outside of his own political and social community subsisted, practically unimpaired, till the rise of the great Empires put an end to the independence of the smaller States, and made men feel that their local gods were too weak to be effective helpers. As a rule communities had one temple and one altar, a single worship of a local god or goddess (Baal and his partner), to whom all sacrifices and vows were addressed, and by whose name all oaths were taken. In addition to this, there were no doubt many minor practices of superstition at sacred wells and trees, or the like; and the higher families might often have teraphim or household idols, to which some form of domestic homage was paid. These minor superstitious [*sic*][5], however, formed no part of the public religion, and could hardly have been associated with the name of any other god than the local Baal, who had to do for his people everything that a god could do for men. There was no room for a differentiation of functions as found in Greece, nor was there much room for ascribing to him any well-marked individuality of character. Every little Canaanite community lived and thought like its neighbours, had the same rounds of daily life, the same needs and wishes to bring before their gods, and the same sacrifice and ritual. Their gods were all cast in the same mould, and were undistinguishable from one another except by their local connections and by separate names. This not only explained polytheism, but also the worship of gods over a wide district beyond the limits of political unity. It was clear on the face of facts that the later Semitic religion was not the direct transcendent [*sic*][6] of Gentile worships [*sic*]. As a rule, the old Gentile faiths survived only in obscure superstitions such as the worship of teraphim, and the full status of God was reserved for the local Baal, who may have originally been identified with the god of a particular clan, but who was essentially the potent god of the place as well as the people. This local god became also the hereditary god of all the inhabitants of the place, because all the gentes traced themselves up to one common stock, as, indeed, the various gentes in one local community habitually learned to do after the establishment of the law of kinship through males. He took it, therefore, that each of the smaller Semitic communities had one god or pair of gods, which were at once gods of the place and hereditary gods of its inhabitants. For the larger Semitic communities the state of religion was not so simple. Such communities were formed in more than one way, and in each case the nature of the political ties had an influence on the national religion. The simplest case was where a homogeneous nation extended its frontiers by conquest or colonisation, and carried the religion along with it. In such cases, as they had seen there was a tendency to break up the national deity into a multitude of local forms. Many of the larger Semitic nations were federations, in which each tribe or city retained its autonomous life, though all acted together for common defence or other specified purposes. They were not called upon to give up their own sanctuaries and gods; but when the people went out to battle together they took their gods with them, and when they met for counsel or celebrated a victory a common religious service could not fail to take place. But the motives to a fusion of religion would naturally be strongest where several cities came to be united, not by a mere federal bond, but under a single kingdom and this was the quarter to which one looked for the beginnings of polytheism in the full sense of the word. The

5.   Should read 'superstitions'.
6.   Misprint for 'descendant'.

polytheism of the Assyrian Empire was admittedly a case in point, though it did not appear that anything like the copious Assyrian pantheon existed in early times in other parts of the Semitic world. When two cities or communes were united by a durable covenant for purposes either of war or commerce, especially when its operation was aided by intermarriage, there would be cases where a member of one community would be the subject of one god and the client of another. This mere clientship did not go far to establish a full polytheistic system, the clearest evidence of developed polytheism being got where in one city there was not merely the temple of one local god, or of a god and goddess, but of several gods and goddesses. They had instructive examples of various gods set up side by side in the history of Solomon and of Ahab, who did so to please their foreign wives, to strengthen the relations of Israel with allied and subject States, and to give the aliens the opportunity to exercise their own religion in Jerusalem, but the innovations were unsuccessful on account of the opposition of the prophets of Northern Israel and the priests at Jerusalem and because the people disliked the foreign ritual. The mass of the Israelites were prone to idolatry and readily accepted all the corruptions of the Canaanite heathenism if they were disguised under the name of Jehovah worship. That the national god would not tolerate a foreign rival within the land was a natural enough deduction from the old Semitic conception of the god as king of the nation—a deduction that could not fail to be drawn wherever there was a strong spirit of national exclusiveness and jealous dislike of foreigners. Discussing the exaggerations of such writers as Baethzen [*sic*][7] as to the polytheism of the nations round about Israel, he said that while it appeared the growth of an extensive practical polytheism among the Northern Semites was but slow, and there was a tendency to acknowledge fewer gods than multiply them, it would be a mistake to ascribe to the national religions any real tendency towards monotheism. Everywhere except in Israel the loss of national independence led to a great spread of polytheism and a free adoption of foreign gods. As to the question whether the plurality of cults was justified by ascribing to each god a distinctive character and a separate function, this was often assumed as a matter of course, apparently for no better reason than that it was so in Greece, and that differentiation of function was the easiest and most obvious explanation of the existence of practical polytheism. But in dealing with times and manners so remote it was unsafe to assume so easy and natural a probability. All the Semitic goddesses were of a highly generalised type, concentrating in themselves, as far as he could make out, all possible divine characters and functions. The chief visible difference between one goddess and another was that in one place the local female deity was associated with a husband, in another with a son, and in a third she was worshipped alone as if unmarried. The Greeks were not more happy in their attempts to find Hellenic gods among the male deities of the Semites. In most cases it was impossible to say why a particular identification was pitched upon, but it was probable that the reason often lay in some tray [*sic*][8] of ritual, as when Plutarch and others concluded from the rites of the Feast of Tabernacles that Bacchus was worshipped by the Jews. The Greek identifications

---

7.   This is a reference to Baethgen.
8.   Should read 'trait'.

proved that the Semitic worship was not absolutely uniform and colourless, but they were not good evidence for ascribing to any Semitic deity a differentiated character corresponding to that of his supposed Hellenic equivalent. For example, it was unsafe to argue, as Baethzen [*sic*][9] did, that the Phoenician Eshmun was a god of healing because the Greeks identified him with Asclepios. He maintained that Eshmun was a great Baal, with the same circle of kingly functions that belonged to other great local Baal [*sic*], that one of these functions was healing; but that this did not distinguish him from other deities, and there was no evidence that the art of healing was specially ascribed to him. The concluding lecture is to be given this afternoon.

The Aberdeen Journal
14th December 1891

The Burnett Lectures

In the Upper Hall of Marischal College, on Saturday afternoon, Professor Robertson Smith delivered the second of the concluding course of his lectures, under the Burnett Trust, on 'The Religious Institutions of the Ancient Semites'. Dealing first with private and public idols, he told of how these were carried from one place to another by the worshippers, and said that particularly was this the case with the latter during times of war, when the object in view—that the god should be always at hand—was attained by the institution of portable sanctuaries, which were to heathenism what the ark was to the Israelites. Proceeding to contrast further than in previous lectures the Semitic religion with that of the Greeks, he showed that the Greeks had access to all the Hellenic gods, while the Semites had no such unity. The Semitic view continued till the rise of the great empires put an end to the small states, bringing home to them that their local gods were not the most powerful. The costly ritual of a polytheistic worship could not be then afforded by these, and, as a rule, such a community had one temple and one altar, and the single worship of the local god or goddess, or both of them together. Many of the larger Semitic nations were federations, in which each factor maintained its original faith, and, though the formation of such union would not call upon those composing it to give up their gods, the league of worshippers implied a league of the gods whom they adored; and, in time, a common worship. A further point of contrast between the two religions was that the Greeks recognised the identity between certain Hellenic and Semitic gods—for example, between Astarte and Aphrodite—but as with the Semites Astarte had a name as widely significant as Baal, there was no differentiation of function, and therefore, from the Semitic point of view, no identity. It was from the Phoenician colonies that the worship of Astarte, the Oriental Aphrodite, spread through Greece, where the nature of her rites marked her out as the goddess of sensual love. But upon Semitic soil this goddess concentrated in herself all possible divine characters and functions. The lecturer concluded by saying that The Greek identification of Ashurun [*sic*][10] with Asclepios was equally unfounded.

9.   See n. 7.
10.   This is an error and should read 'Eshmun'.

Third Series, Lecture 3: The Gods and the World: Cosmogony

The Daily Free Press
Tuesday, December 15, 1891

The Burnett Lectures
Dr Robertson Smith on Semetic [sic] Cosmogony

Professor Robertson Smith concluded his final series of Burnett lectures on Semitic Religion in the Hall of Marischal College yesterday. There was a fairly large audience. At the outset the lecturer said he proposed that day to speak on the Semitic cosmogony—on the opinions entertained by the Semites as to the origin of the gods and of the world. Proceeding to do so, he quoted, in the first place, from Mr Andrew Lang—whom he described as one of the best general anthropologists of the day—as to the origin of the world and of men being a problem which had naturally exercised the curiosity of the least developed minds, and as to the varying theories upon the subject that were entertained by the various races. These general remarks, he said, would be useful to them in looking specially at the fragments of Semitic cosmogony that had come down to them, and would serve as a warning not to seek too much of a consistency in the beliefs as to the origin of the Universe and of man. In this regard it was to be at once observed that the simple and grand cosmogony of the First Chapter of Genesis had no parallel amongst the ancient Semites, because none of them had such a conception of God as the sole creator of the world. In a complete cosmogony they should expect to find three main topics treated; first, the origin of heaven and earth; second, the origin of the gods; and, thirdly, the origin of man. They must not expect, however, to find all these topics embraced in every cosmogonic story. Among the Arabs he found a Myth as to the origin of heaven and earth; and again, as regarded the origin of the gods, all the Semites thought of the gods as begetting and begotten, and must, therefore have had the rudiments of a Theogony. Finally, as regarded the origin of man, they did not always find a theory of the origin of mankind as a whole, but only special theories held by individual tribes as regarded their own origin. Cosmogonic myths did not generally spring from any wide philosophical view of the universe, but owed their origin to local stories invented by a narrow circle to account for its own existence and surroundings. Coming now to the main subject of the lecture, Professor Smith went on to discuss in detail, first, the Chaldean cosmogony in its Babylonish form, chiefly as illustrated by the Syrian [sic][11] tablets now in the British Museum; and second, the Phoenician cosmogony, contrasting both with the cosmogony of the Hebrew race. In dealing with the Chaldean record, he pointed out that the tablets were inscribed about a generation after Isaiah prophesied, but the story they contained was very much older—it was not safe to say how much older, but no doubt it was the most ancient cosmogonic story in the world. The record was very imperfect and hard to understand, but much was made clear to them by comparing that record with others. He thought a very great deal too much was some-

11. This should read 'Assyrian'.

times made of the entirely new light they were sometimes said to have derived from those tablets. In everything except the simple historical inscriptions, it seemed to him they were almost wholly unable to interpret what was in the tablets; and with regard to the theory of the creation and the flood and so forth, he did not think they could have made anything of the cuneiform [*sic*] inscriptions without assistance from Greek sources. As to the Babylonish Creation story itself, he pointed out that the Hebrew account of the Creation bore the title, 'These are the generations of the heaven and the earth,' and it was summed up in the words, 'So the heaven and the earth were finished.' In like manner the generations of the heaven and the earth, or the making of heaven and earth and their denizens, would fairly sum up the contents of the Babylonish Creation legend. Entering still further on a consideration of the Babylonish theory, he pointed out that, like that of the Hebrews, it accepted the 'visible firmament' to mean the dome that was spread over the habitable globe 'like a tent to dwell in,' as Isaiah said, and that both theories taught that beyond this dome were waters that would fall upon the earth and submerge it if the windows of heaven were opened. Waters also extended all round and beneath the earth. Cosmogony, therefore, upon the old Semitic view was an enclosed space between the outspread earth and the domed heaven, surrounded on all sides by water, an unlimited extent of water, and the problem of creation was to understand how this region separated from the dark primordial ocean, and instinct with light life, took its beginnings. The Chaldean theory assumed that the primordial ocean existed in the beginning before the gods were shaped, before the heaven and earth existed. The gods of the upper and lower world alike, according to this theory, sprang from the being with the monstrous brood, the original Chaos, and the heaven and the earth took their origin from the destruction of this being—one half going to form the heaven and the other half the earth. Life still had to be created, at least upon the earth, and it was recorded how Baal [*sic*][12] fashioned the sun and stars, the moon, and the seven planets. The monstrous brood of Chaos could not bear the light that now appeared, and there now arose an entirely new creation. Such was the Chaldean cosmogony in its Babylonish form, and he thought they would at once agree that the parallel drawn between it and the first chapter of Genesis, on which many recent writers laid great stress, had been much exaggerated. The main point of agreement was that both accounts began with a dark chaos, but in the Babylonish theory the chaos was productive, and in the Bible story the chaos was only the raw material of creation, from which the orderly elements of Cosmos were separated by the creative Word of God. It would be seen that the Babylonish theory was not therefore so very like that in the Bible as was supposed; on the other hand, it was closely akin to the myths of savage nations. Coming now to the Phoenician cosmogony, he said the first matter to be noticed in it was the theory of the origin of heaven and earth. The best established point in this regard was that the world came into being by the bursting in twain of a cosmogonic egg, one piece of which became heaven and the other earth. The egg was supposed to be a watery mass, but contained the germs of life—in this theory life was instinct, whereas in the Hebrew cosmogony life was created directly by the word of God. The Phoenicians had something to say

---

12.   This should read 'Bel' (i.e., Marduk).

about the origin of the world-egg, but the accounts varied, some of them introducing metaphysical conceptions like time and desire, but all the accounts agreed in a remarkable way in making the egg be preceded by the winds or by a murky, turbid darkness. The primeval world seemed to have been conceived as having been subjected to the action of the winds on a dark, misty chaos, and here they had a parallel of the brooding of the spirit—or wind—of God upon the face of the deep. The lecturer then went on to select for special treatment some of the more characteristic and interesting points of the Phoenician cosmogny [*sic*] especially, still comparing the various theories with corresponding points in the Hebrew belief. One of the most characteristic mentioned was the local colouring imparted to the mythical conception, and in this regard he pointed out that in the scenery of the Garden of Eden and all its details, which must be treated allegorically if they were to attach to it a spiritual meaning, they had in great part the scenery of a Phoenician sanctuary. To these, various things might be added from other sources. For example, it was very probable that Justin XVIII, who speaks of the Phoenicians being driven from their first seats by earthquake, and having dwelt by the Assyrian lake before they settled on the Sidonian shore, might refer to the destruction of Sodom and Gomorrah. Or again, as Noah in the Bible was the first to plant the vine, so the Tyrians had a legend of the god Dionysus first teaching a Phoenician shepherd the use of the grape. All this showed that Phoenician and Hebrew legend covered much the same general ground; but the similarity in material details only brought out into more emphasis the entire difference of spirit and meaning. The Phoenician legends were bound up throughout with a thoroughly heathen view of God, man, and the world. Not merely were they destitute of ethical motives; but no one who believed them could rise to any spiritual conception of deity or any lofty conception of man's chief end. The Hebrew stories in Genesis, looked at in their plain sense, contained much that was not directly edifying. They did not make the patriarchs models of goodness, but they never made religion involve the approbation of a lower morality or a low view of the deity. In them God communed with men without even [*sic*][13] lowering Himself to the level of man. He had no human passions or affections, for His love to His chosen people was raised far above the weaknesses of human preferences. Above all, he was the God of the world before He was Israel's God; while in all the Semitic legends, the Demiurge himself was always, and above all, the local king. The burden of explaining this contrast did not lie with him: it fell on those who were compelled by a false philosophy of revelation to see in the Old Testament nothing more than the highest fruit of the general tendencies of Semitic religion. That was not the view that study commended to him. It was a view that was not commended but condemned by the many parallelisms in detail between the Hebrew and heathen story and ritual, for all the material points of resemblance only made the contrast in spirit more remarkable— (loud applause).

Sir John Clark of Tillypronie, one of the Burnett Trustees, said it would naturally have fallen to him, as by seniority the chairman of the Burnett Trust, to move a vote of thanks to Professor Robertson Smith for the able, interesting, and laboriously con-

---

13.   An error for 'ever'.

scientious course of lectures which he had now concluded. His fellow-trustees and he felt, however, that really to do justice to the learning of these lectures it required an expert in the same sphere of inquiry as Professor Robertson Smith himself, and accordingly they had asked Professor Kennedy to discharge the duty. But, before calling on Professor Kennedy, he should ask Dr Bain, his co-trustee, to make a reference to the late Dr Webster, the revered chairman, the father of the Burnett Trust.

Dr Bain, in responding, said it fell to him to make some remarks at the close of this second[14] course of lectures on the Burnett foundation. In doing so, he took the place that would have been filled by his lamented colleague, the senior member of the Trust. His first duty then was to recall the important part that Dr Webster played in the history of the Trust for the last forty years. His father preceded him in the management, and conducted the first Prize Essay competition in 1814. The second competition, in 1854, fell to the son, and could be remembered by many of them. He left nothing undone on the occasion to make it a success; his choice of examiner was painstaking and unexceptionable. Talking over the first occasion, no doubt, with his father, and cogitating on his experience of the second, he seemed to have concluded that some better model could be found of attaining the object of the testator; and when the Act of 1878 for remodelling Scotch Endowments was passed, he drafted a proposal for a Lectureship, to be administered by the three trustees and two assessors, as was generally known. His heart was still in the work, and he omitted no effort on his part to make the Lectureship more successful than the Prize Essays had been. They had now heard the conclusion of the second [*sic*][15] course, and would admit that it did honour to the distinguished lecturer and credit to their choice as a body— (applause). They had hoped that Dr Webster would have been there to see its conclusion and would also have taken part in the election of Dr Smith's successor, which was ordained for the present year. That election was postponed by his death, until his place in the Trust was filled up, as it had happily been by the appointment of one of the foremost men in the affairs of the city, whether in his official capacity, or in his administration of our most important charitable institution. By this appointment they were enabled to proceed to the nomination of the next lecturer, and, as they knew, their choice fell upon Dr William Davidson, minister of Bourtie. Only one of the two assessors—Professor Flint—could be present: Dr Edmond was prevented by infirmity from taking part, but they had the satisfaction of having his concurrence in their choice, which rendered it unanimous. Dr Davidson would give two courses of six lectures each on the two next following winters, being contemporary with the Gifford lecturer just appointed. The courses would be kept distinct in time, and their arrangement would have to follow the announcement of Principal Fairbairn's understanding with the Senatus—(applause).

Professor Kennedy, in moving thanks to the lecturer, said he was very glad to be able to express his own indebtedness and the indebtedness of the younger generation of Old Testament students to Professor Smith. The younger men owed much directly to Professor Smith for the inspiration of his works—(applause)—but they owed far

14.   This should read 'third'.
15.   See note 14 above.

more to him indirectly, for they saw in him the victorious champion of free research in the Old Testament—(loud applause). It was now a matter of ancient history, and he need not recall the days when Professor Smith had to fight for freedom of research. They knew that the nominal victory was with his opponents, but the moral victory was his—and remained his—(renewed applause)—and the loss, as every day was more and more showing, was theirs, was Scotland's, and above all, he made bold to say, was that of the Church of which he was such a brilliant ornament—(applause). Coming to the subject of the lectures, he said he was not called on to criticise them, even were he competent to do so, which he was not, but he wished to reiterate what was said by Dr Bain, who indeed had anticipated him in this, that the Burnett Trustees, in asking Dr Robertson Smith, and inducing him to leave his scholarly retreat in the great University which welcomed with open arms their Scottish outcast, had earned the gratitude of the Republic—the whole Republic of Semitic students—(loud applause). He said, and he said advisedly, that a debt of gratitude was owing to the Burnett Trustees for bringing down Dr Robertson Smith to Aberdeen, and for being the means of letting the great public know what Dr Robertson Smith had to say about the origin of Semitic religion—(applause). He already said he was not going to discuss these lectures—perhaps some of them having a leaning towards theological study thought Professor Smith had not perhaps done justice to their favourite subject. But that was by the way. He wished only to allude to a single aspect of the lectures which did not perhaps impress itself upon them all. It was suggested in Professor Smith's closing words—he meant the Apologetic aspect. It was every day becoming more and more apparent that for full apprehension of the great doctrine of their own most holy religion it was more and more necessary to go back to that religion in which Christianity had its root, and they saw when they studied the Hebrew ritual that even there they were not, as it were, at the root of the matter, but had to go back to the primitive religion of the Semites, the great stock from which the Hebrew sprang, and those who had studied carefully—as he had striven to do—Professor Smith's former course would see that they could not attain to a full grasp of the great doctrine of the Atonement until they had gone back and followed Dr Robertson Smith in his exposition of the primitive doctrine of Semitic sacrifice.

The vote of thanks was passed amid hearty applause, and Professor Smith returned his thanks.

The Aberdeen Journal
15th December 1891

The Burnett Lectures

Yesterday afternoon the third and concluding lecture of the second course under the auspices of the Burnett Trust was delivered in the Upper Hall of Marischal College, by Professor Robertson Smith, on 'The Religious Institutions of the Ancient Semites.' Among those present were—Principal Geddes, Dr Bain, Professor Stewart, Professor Kennedy, Sir John F. Clark of Tillypronie, Professor Pirie, Professor Robertson, &c. The learned professor began by saying that the subject he intended to treat was the opinions entertained by the Semites of the origin and cause of the world. The subject of the origin of the world and of men was naturally a problem which had exercised the curiosity of the least developed minds. Having referred in some detail to the legends and myths of heathen nations, he said such a summary would be useful in looking at the fragments of Semitic cosmics, and might serve to warn them not to seek too much, nor to build out of the Babylonian records a single consistent picture of the origin of the universe and of man. The grand cosmogony of the first chapter of Genesis, he said, had no parallel in the heathen cosmogony, although the pictorial details had some resemblance to the Babylonian myths. The lesson of the story of the Creation, however, was entirely foreign to heathenism. In the Old Testament the doctrine of one God the Creator of all was one of the chief cornerstones of practical religion, whereas among the heathen the origin of the world was a matter of mere curiosity. In all cosmogonies they might expect to find three things—(1) the origin of heaven and earth; (2) the origin of the gods; and (3) the origin of man. He warned his hearers, however, that, as to these points, and especially with regard to the origin of man, they should not always find the theory as a whole, but only special theories held by individual tribes. The learned professor then dealt with the myths contained in the Babylonian tablets in the British Museum, warning his audience that too much had been made of these tablets, and especially of the legends contained in them of the Creation and the Flood. The heathen Babylonians, like the Hebrews, understood the visible firmament as a dome spread over the habitable earth, like a tent, to dwell in. To both nations the dome of heaven was a solid sphere, in which the heavenly bodies moved. Above the solid dome there were waters, and, if the windows of heaven were opened, the waters would fall upon the earth and submerge it. As there were waters above the heavens so the earth rested upon water, which extended all round and beneath the earth. Having entered in further detail upon these myths the lecturer proceeded to discuss the Chaldean cosmogony in its Babylonian form, and drew a parallel between that cosmogony and the first chapter of Genesis. That parallel, he asserted, had been much exaggerated. The main point of agreement was that both accounts began with a dark chaos, but as regarded the steps of the Creation he was unable to find any parallel. The learned professor then passed on to deal with the Phoenician myths, stating that the best established version of the Creation was that the world came into being by the bursting in twain of a cosmic egg; and he afterwards proceeded to discuss the connection of particular persons in the Theogony with the invention of useful arts and with forms of religious observance. In the Phoenician story of the Garden of Eden there was the tree, the serpent, and the flaming sword, and the Hebrew story bore all the colour of that version, though it put a new meaning into it. After discussing the parallel between the Phoenician legends and the oldest narrative of Genesis, he said that they both covered very much the same general ground, but that the similarity only brought out with more emphasis the entire difference of the spirit and meaning. The Phoenician legends were bound up with an utterly heathen view of God and the world, and were destitute of ethical motives, and never rose to any spiritual conception of Deity.

Sir John Clark, Bart., the chairman of the Burnett Trustees, asked Professor Kennedy to propose a vote of thanks to the lecturer, but before doing so mentioned that he had intended to express on behalf of his colleagues, their sense of the great loss they had sustained in the death of Dr Webster. He had found, however, that Dr Bain had intended to do so, and before calling upon Professor Kennedy he asked Dr Bain to speak.

Dr Bain, in responding, said it fell to him to make some remarks at the close of this second [*sic*][16] course of lectures on the Burnett foundation. In doing so, he took the place that would have been filled by his lamented colleague, the senior member of the trust. His first duty, then, was to recall the important part that Dr Webster played in the history of the trust for the last 40 years. His father preceded him in the management, and conducted the first prize essay competition in 1814. The second competition, in 1854, fell to the son, and could be remembered by many of them. He left nothing undone on the occasion to make it a success; his choice of examiner was painstaking and unexceptionable. Talking over the first occasion, no doubt, with his father, and cogitating on his experience of the second, he seemed to have concluded that some better mode could be found of attaining the object of the testator; and when the Act of 1878 for remodelling Scotch endowments was passed, he drafted a proposal for a lectureship, to be administered by the three trustees and two assessors, as was generally known. His heart was still in the work, and he omitted no effort on his part to make the lectureship more successful than the prize essays had been. They had now heard the conclusion of the second [*sic*][17] course, and would admit that it did honour to the distinguished lecturer and credit to their choice as a body. (Applause.) They had hoped that Dr Webster would have been there to see its conclusion, and would also have taken part in the election of Dr Smith's successor, which was ordained for the present year. That election was postponed by his death, until his place in the trust was filled up, as it had happily been by the appointment of one of the foremost men in the affairs of the city, whether in his official capacity, or in his administration of our most important charitable institution. By this appointment they were enabled to proceed to the nomination of the next lecturer, and as they knew, their choice fell upon Dr William Davidson, minister of Bourtie. Only one of the two assessors—Professor Flint—could be present; Dr Edmond was prevented by infirmity from taking part, but they had the satisfaction of having his concurrence in their choice, which rendered it unanimous. Dr Davidson would give two courses of six lectures each on the two next following winters, being contemporary with the Gifford lecturer just appointed. The courses would be kept distinct in time, and their arrangement would have to follow the announcement of Principal Fairbairn's understanding with the Senatus. (Applause.)

Professor Kennedy, in moving a vote of thanks to Professor Smith, expressed his own indebtedness and that of the younger generation of Old Testament students. The younger men owed much directly to Professor Smith for the inspiration of his books, but they owed far more indirectly for they saw in him the victorious champion of free research in the Old Testament. (Applause.) It was now a matter of ancient history, and he need not recall the contest when he had to fight for freedom of research. They

16. See n. 14.
17. See n. 14.

knew that the nominal victory was with his opponents, but the moral victory was his, and remained his. (Applause.) The loss, as every day had more fully shown, was theirs—was Scotland's—and, above all, he would make bold to say, was a loss to a Church of which he was such a brilliant ornament. Dealing with the subject of the lectures, Professor Kennedy proceeded to express the gratitude of the whole republic of Semitic students to the Burnett Trustees for bringing down Professor Robertson Smith. In the course of his further remarks, he said they could not attain to a full grasp of the great doctrine of the Atonement until they had gone back and followed Robertson Smith in his exposition of the primitive doctrine of Semitic sacrifice. He moved a vote of thanks to Professor Smith for the able and luminous course which he had just brought to a close. (Applause.)

Professor Smith, in a word, acknowledged.

BIBLIOGRAPHY*

Baethgen, F., *Beiträge zur semitischen Religionsgeschichte* (Berlin: H. Reuther, 1888).

Barr, J., 'Philo of Byblos and his "Phoenician history"', *BJRL* 57 (1974), pp. 17-68.

Black, J.S. and G. Chrystal (eds.), *Lectures & Essays of William Robertson Smith* (London: A. & C. Black, 1912).

—*The Life of William Robertson Smith* (London: A. & C. Black, 1912).

Blunt, A., *Bedouin Tribes of the Euphrates* (2 vols.; London: John Murray, 1879).

Bochart, S., *Geographia Sacra seu Phaleg et Canaan* (Leiden: C. Bontesteyn & J. Luchtmans, 4th edn, 1707).

Bouché-Leclercq, A., *L'histoire de la Divination dans l'antiquité* (4 vols.; Paris: E. Leroux, 1879–82).

Budde, K., *Die biblische Urgeschichte* (Giessen: J. Ricker, 1883).

—Review of W.R. Smith, *Lectures on the Religion of the Semites* (1st series, 2nd edn), in *TLZ* 20, no. 22 (26 October, 1895), cols. 553-54.

—Review of the second edition of *The Religion of the Semites*, translated in 'British Table Talk', in *The British Weekly* 19, no. 470 (31 October, 1895), p. 21.

Cassuto, U., *A Commentary on the Book of Genesis. Part I: From Adam to Noah* (Jerusalem: Magnes, 1961).

Clermont-Ganneau, C., *Recueil d'archéologie orientale* (8 vols.; Paris: E. Leroux, 1888).

Cureton, W., *Spicilegium Syriacum* (London: Rivingtons, 1855).

Daremberg, C. and E. Saglio (eds.), *Dictionnaire des antiquités grecques et romaines* (5 vols. in 10; Paris: Hachette, 1877–1919).

Davie, G.E., *The Scottish Enlightenment and other Essays* (Edinburgh: Polygon, 1991).

Day, J., *God's Conflict with the Dragon and the Sea* (Cambridge: Cambridge University Press, 1985).

—'William Robertson Smith's hitherto unpublished second and third series of Burnett lectures on the Religion of the Semites', in W. Johnstone (ed.), *William Robertson Smith: Essays in Reassessment* (JSOTSup, 189; Sheffield: Sheffield Academic Press, 1995), pp. 190-202.

Dillmann, A., *Der Prophet Jesaia* (Leipzig: S. Hirzel, 1890).

—'Über das Kalenderwesen der Israeliten vor dem babylonischen Exil', in *Monatsberichte der königlichen preussischen Akademie der Wissenschaften zu Berlin 1881* (1882), pp. 914-35.

Doughty, C.M., *Travels in Arabia Deserta* (2 vols.; Cambridge: Cambridge University Press, 1888).

---

* This bibliography includes works cited not only in Robertson Smith's work but also in John Day's Introduction to it.

Ebach, J., *Weltentstehung und Kulturentwicklung bei Philo von Byblos* (BWANT 108; Stuttgart: W. Kohlhammer, 1979).

Flügel, G. (ed.), *Kitâb al-Fihrist* (Leipzig: F.C.W. Vogel, 1871).

Geraty, L.T., 'Baalis', in D.N. Freedman (ed.), *Anchor Bible Dictionary* 1 (New York: Doubleday, 1992), pp. 556-57.

Halévy, J., *Mélanges de critique et d'histoire relatifs aux peuples sémitiques* (Paris: Maisonneuve, 1883).

Head, B.V., *Historia Numorum* (Oxford: Clarendon Press, 1887).

Hoffmann, J.G.E., *Opuscula Nestoriana* (Kiel: G. von Maack; Paris: Maisonneuve, 1880).

Houston, W.J., *Purity and Monotheism: Clean and Unclean Animals in Biblical Law* (JSOTSup 140; Sheffield: JSOT Press, 1993).

Jensen, P., *Die Kosmologie der Babylonier* (Strasbourg: K.J. Trübner, 1890).

Kaibel, G. (ed.), *Inscriptiones Italiae et Siciliae* (Inscriptiones Graecae XIV; Berlin: G. Reimarus, 1890).

Lagarde, P.A.H. de, *Onomastica Sacra* (Göttingen: A. Rente, 1870);

—*Orientalia* (2 vols.; Göttingen: Dieterich, 1879–80).

Lang, A., *Myth, Ritual, and Religion* (2 vols.; London: Longmans, Green, 1887).

Le Bas, P. and W.H. Waddington, *Voyage archéologique en Grèce et en Asie Mineure* (Paris: Didot, 1870).

Lemaire, A., 'Déesses et dieux de Syrie-Palestine d'après les inscriptions (c. 1000–500 av. n.è.)', in W. Dietrich and M.A. Klopfenstein, *Ein Gott allein?* (Kolloquium der Schweizerischen Akademie der Geistes- und Socialwissenschaften 1993; Freiburg: Universitätsverlag, 1994), pp. 127-58.

Lindsay, T.M., 'Pioneer and Martyr of the Higher Criticism: Professor William Robertson Smith', *The Review of the Churches* 6 (1894), pp. 37-42.

Lotz, W. (ed.), *Die Inschriften Tiglathpileser's, I* (Leipzig: J.C. Hinrichs, 1880).

Martin, M. L'Abbé, 'Discours de Jacques de Saroug sur la chute des idoles', *ZDMG* 29 (1875).

Meyer, E., 'Ueber einige semitische Götter', *ZDMG* 31 (1877), pp. 716-41.

Migne, J.-P., *Patrologiae cursus completus. Series Graeca* (161 vols.; Paris: J.-P. Migne: 1857–66).

—*Patrologiae cursus completus. Series Latina* (221 vols.; Paris: J.-P. Migne, 1844–63).

Movers, F.K., *Die Phönizier* (2 vols. in 4; Bonn: E. Weber; Berlin: F. Dümmler, 1841–56).

Müller, C. (ed.), *Fragmenta historicorum Graecorum* (5 vols.; Paris: Didot, 1841–70).

Muqadassī, *Descriptio imperii Moslemici (Ahsan al-Taqāsīm fī Ma'rifat al-Aqālim)* (ed. M.J. de Goeje; Bibliotheca geographorum Arabicorum 3; Leiden: E.J. Brill, 1877 [ET Mukaddasi (ed. G. Le Strange), *Description of Syria including Palestine* (London: Palestine Pilgrim's Text Society, 1886)].

Nicholson, E.W., 'Israelite Religion in the pre-exilic period', in J.D. Martin and P.R. Davies (eds.), *A Word in Season: Essays in honour of William McKane* (JSOTSup 42; Sheffield: JSOT Press, 1986), pp. 3-34.

Nöldeke, T., review of Baethgen's *Beiträge zur semitischen Religionsgeschichte*, *ZDMG* 42 (1888), 470-87.

—'Zwei goldene Kameele als Votivgeschenke bei Arabern', *ZDMG* 38 (1884), pp. 143-44.

Orelli, J.C. von, *Sanchoniathonis Berytii quae feruntur fragmenta de Cosmogonia et Theologia Phoenicum* (Leipzig: Hinrichs, 1826).

Perrot, G. and C. Chipiez, *Histoire de l'Art* (10 vols.; Paris: Hachette, 1882–1914).

Pietschmann, R., *Geschichte der Phönizier* (Berlin: G. Grote, 1889).

Pinches, T.G., 'A new Version of the Creation-story', *JRAS* 23 (1891), pp. 393-408.

Renan, E., *Mission de Phénicie* (Paris: Imprimerie Impériale, 1864).

Ruelle, C.A. [E.] (ed.), *Damascii successoris dubitationes et solutiones de primis principiis* (2 vols.; Paris: C. Klincksieck, 1889).

Sachau, C.E. (ed.), *Chronologie orientalischer Völker von Albêrûnî* (Leipzig: F.A. Brockhaus, 1878).

—(ed.), *The chronology of ancient nations. An English version of the Arabic text of the Athâr-ul-bâkiya of Albîrûnî* (London: W.H. Allen, 1879).

Schrader, E., 'Assyrisch-babylonisches. 3.', *Jahrbücher für protestantische Theologie* 1 (1875), pp. 334-38.

—*Die Keilinschriften und das Alte Testament* (Giessen: J. Ricker, 2nd edn, 1883).

—(ed.), *Keilinschriftliche Bibliothek* (3 vols. in 1; Berlin: H. Reuther, 1889–90).

Smith, W.R., 'Moloch' in *Encyclopaedia Britannica* XVI (Edinburgh: A. & C. Black, 9th edn, 1883), pp. 695-96.

—'On the forms of divination and magic enumerated in Deut. XVIII.10,11', *Journal of Philology* 13 (1885), pp. 273-87, and 14 (1885), pp. 113-28.

—'Palmyra', in *Encyclopaedia Britannica* XVIII (Edinburgh: A. & C. Black, 9th edn, 1885), pp. 198-203.

—'Priest', in *Encyclopaedia Britannica* XIX (Edinburgh: A. & C. Black, 9th edn, 1885), pp. 724-30.

—'Prophet', in *Encyclopaedia Britannica* XIX (Edinburgh: A. & C. Black, 9th edn, 1885), pp. 814-22.

—'Semiramis', in *Encyclopaedia Britannica* XXI (Edinburgh: A. & C. Black, 9th edn, 1886), pp. 639-40.

—'Ctesias and the Semiramis Legend', *English Historical Review* 2.6 (April, 1887), pp. 303-17.

—'Tabernacles, feast of', in *Encyclopaedia Britannica* XXIII (Edinburgh: A. & C. Black, 9th edn, 1888), p. 6.

—*Lectures on the Religion of the Semites* (Edinburgh: A. & C. Black, 1st series, 1st edn., 1889; 2nd edn, 1894; 3rd edn, 1927).

—'Prophecy and Personality', 'The question of prophecy in the critical schools of the continent', 'The fulfilment of prophecy', and 'Two lectures on prophecy', in J.S. Black and G. Chrystal (eds.), *Lectures & Essays of William Robertson Smith*, pp. 97-108, 163-203, 253-84, and 341-66.

Spencer, J., *De Legibus Hebraeorum Ritualibus* (2 vols.; Cambridge: Typis Academicis, 1727).

Tiele, C.P., *Babylonisch-assyrische Geschichte* (2 vols.; Gotha: F.A. Perthes, 1888).

Tigay, J., *You shall have no other gods* (Atlanta: Scholars, 1986).

Vogüé, C.J.M. de, 'Inscriptions phéniciennes d l'île de Cypre', *Journal Asiatique* 10 (1867), pp. 85-176.

—*Mélanges d'archéologie orientale* (Paris: Imprimerie impériale, 1868).

Wellhausen, J., *Prolegomena zur Geschichte Israels* (Berlin: G. Reimer, 1883 [ET *Prolegomena to the History of Israel*; Edinburgh: A & C. Black, 1885]).

—*Reste arabischen Heidentumes* (Skizzen und Vorarbeiten III; Berlin: G. Reimer, 1887);

Wenham, G.J., 'Sanctuary symbolism in the garden of Eden story', in *Proceedings of the Ninth World Congress of Jewish Studies: Division A. The Period of the Bible* (Jerusalem: World Union of Jewish Studies, 1986), pp. 19-25.

Wright, W. (ed.), *The Chronicle of Joshua the Stylite* (Cambridge: Cambridge University Press, 1882).

INDEXES

INDEX OF BIBLICAL REFERENCES

OLD TESTAMENT

Genesis		28.35	53	21.1-9	48
1	26, 29, 97, 102, 103	30.12-16	47	23.4	82
		32.1	49	31.25	50
1.2	27, 100	33.6	50	33.2	67
1.7	99	33.7	49	33.8-11	49
1.14	35	33.11	50	33.8	49, 50
2–3	28	33.20	50		
2.1	99	34.18	19	*Joshua*	
2.4	99	34.22	36, 37, 40	7	44
3	28			11.17	23
4.17-26	27	*Leviticus*		12.7	23
4.17	28, 107	23	37	13.5	23
4.20-22	28, 107	23.9	40		
6.1-4	111	23.24	35, 36	*Judges*	
7.4	19, 43	23.42	36	3.3	23
7.11	19, 42, 99, 100			5.4	67
		Numbers		6.26	46
8.3-4	43	5.11-31	48	6.28	46
8.14-16	43	12	49, 50	9.4	48
28.20-22	73	12.8	50	9.27	36
31.30	74	25.1-3	25, 86	10.6	88
33.20	67	25.14	86	13.15-20	46
35	67	25.18	86	16.21-23	85
		29.6	40	16.23	79
Exodus				17–18	48
13.4	19	*Deuteronomy*		18.17-20	20, 49
18.19	50	13.1-3	57	18.30	75
19.23	48	16.1	19, 36	21.19	36
20.22-26	20, 46	16.3	40		
21.6	49	16.9	40	*1 Samuel*	
22.8-9	49	16.13	36	2.12-17	45
23.15	19	17.11	51	2.22	37
23.16	35, 37, 40	18	125	2.25	49
23.18	40	18.9-19	56	4.1–7.2	49
23.19	40	18.10-11	21, 55	5	85
23.26	36	18.21-22	57	6.7	51

INDEX OF AUTHORS

JOURNAL FOR THE STUDY OF THE OLD TESTAMENT

Supplement Series